8.95
5.1.71

RURAL TRANSPORT
IN DEVELOPING COUNTRIES

The World Employment Programme (WEP) was launched by the International Labour Organisation in 1969, as the ILO's main contribution to the International Development Strategy for the Second United Nations Development Decade.

The means of action adopted by the WEP have included the following:
— short-term high-level advisory missions;
— longer-term national or regional employment teams; and
— a wide-ranging research programme.

Through these activities the ILO has been able to help national decision-makers to reshape their policies and plans with the aim of eradicating mass poverty and unemployment.

A landmark in the development of the WEP was the World Employment Conference of 1976, which proclaimed *inter alia* that 'strategies and national development plans should include as a priority objective the promotion of employment and the satisfaction of the basic needs of each country's population'. The Declaration of Principles and Programme of action adopted by the Conference will remain the cornerstone of WEP technical assistance and research activities during the 1980s.

This publication is the outcome of a WEP project.

RURAL TRANSPORT
IN DEVELOPING COUNTRIES

I. J. BARWELL, G. A. EDMONDS, J. D. G. F. HOWE and
J. DE VEEN

*A study prepared for the International Labour Office
within the framework of the World Employment Programme*

INTERMEDIATE TECHNOLOGY PUBLICATIONS 1985

Copyright © International Labour Organisation 1985

Published by Intermediate Technology Publications Ltd.
9 King Street, London WC2E 8HN, UK

ISBN 0 946688 80 X

Printed in Great Britain by Billings, Worcester

The responsibility for opinions expressed in studies and other contributions rests solely with their authors, and publication does not constitute an endorsement by the International Labour Office of the opinions expressed in them.

References to firm names and commercial products and processes do not imply the endorsement of the International Labour Office, and any failure to mention a particular firm, commercial product or process in connection with the technologies described in this volume is not a sign of disapproval.

The designations employed and the presentation of material do not imply the expression of any opinion whatsoever on the part of the International Labour Office concerning the legal status of any country or territory or of its authorities, or concerning the delimitation of its frontiers.

CONTENTS

	Page
ILO FOREWORD	1
EDITORS' INTRODUCTION	2

PART I — TRANSPORT PATTERNS — 5
   CHAPTER 1 — Small holder Transport Requirements in Malaysia — 5
   CHAPTER 2 — Rural Transport in India — 21
   CHAPTER 3 — Rural Transport in Northern Nigeria — 34
   CHAPTER 4 — Transport in Two Kenyan Villages — 48

PART II — TRANSPORT MEANS — 61
   CHAPTER 5 — Means of Transport in Western Samoa — 61
   CHAPTER 6 — Improving Tranditional Means of Transport in the Republic of Korea — 71
   CHAPTER 7 — Means of Transport in the Philippines — 77

PART III — TRANSPORT POLICIES — 93
   CHAPTER 8 — Transport in a Rural Community in Tanzania — 93
   CHAPTER 9 — Bangaladesh Rural Transport Study — 109
   CHAPTER 10 — Transport for Small Farmers in Kenya — 118

PART IV — SUMMARY — 127
   CHAPTER 11 — Conclusions and Policy Implications — 127
   CHAPTER REFERENCES — 139
   SELECTED BIBLIOGRAPHY — 144

The publishers wish to thank the following for use of their photographs:

United Nations Association for Plate 1; Dr Seyeul Kim for Plates 5 and 7.

The other plates have been provided by the authors, the International Labour Office and from the Intermediate Technology Transport Archives.

ILO Foreword

Rural transport is one of the most significant means of ensuring that those who live in rural areas have access to markets for their products and to social services. While much has been published — by the ILO, the World Bank and others — on rural access roads, little has been written on alternative means of rural transport. The present volume, edited by Messrs. Barwell, Edmonds, Howe and de Veen, is designed to fill this gap. Research work in support of the volume was undertaken within the framework of the ILO Technology and Employment Programme, and was financed by a research grant from the Swedish Government (Swedish Agency for Research Co-operation with Development Countries — SAREC).

The volume contains a selection of case studies which highlight transport patterns, means and policies. One of the main conclusions of the study is that transport planning in most developing countries takes insufficient account of the needs and requirements of the bulk of the rural population. Only the transport demands of a few large farmers producing for the export markets are captured by conventional transport planning; the transport needs of the rest of the rural population are largely for the movement of small loads over relatively short distances and this is largely ignored. In addition poor credit facilities are a major constraint on the small producer acquiring even simple means of transport.

Within the framework of the United National Administrative Committee on Co-ordination Task Force on Science and Technology for Development, a number of joint activities have been formulated for implementation at the country level in the Third World. Upgrading of traditional transport technology is one such activity for which the ILO has been designated as a lead agency. The present volume is a contribution to this programme — which it is envisaged will also include a selected number of operational projects within the developing countries.

A.S. BHALLA,
Chief, Technology and Employment Branch

Introduction

For more than three decades investment in the transport sector has been a priority for developing country governments. With a few exceptions, roads have accounted for the major part of these investments. The explicit, and often articulated, assumption upon which the decision to allocate such large sums of money to road transport has been made is that road transport and development are inextricably linked. The implicit, and rarely articulated assumption is that the provision of suitable roads will lead to the operation of an adequate level of road transport services. If roads do not actually produce economic development, it has been argued, they certainly play a major role. This belief in the beneficial effects of roads is not wholly unsubstantiated. Clearly the provision of some form of access is vital for the development of the rural economy. Nevertheless, the studies carried out over the last 10-15 years on the impact of highway investment have sounded a cautionary note. George W. Wilson, writing in the concluding chapter of the Brookings Institution studies on transport and development, suggested that* 'A much more sceptical attitude towards transport appears essential and far more attention needs to be devoted to the set of circumstances surrounding expansion of transport capacity'.[1] The suggestion of a more restrained attitude reflected a growing concern that transport, and in particular roads, was only one factor amongst a large number that needed to be integrated for effective development. The concern to see road transport in a wider context partly explains the move towards the evaluation of the social, as well as strictly economic, benefits of road construction.

More recently the argument about the role of transport in development has largely been overshadowed by the practicalities of the situation. The effect of new roads becomes somewhat academic if funds are not forthcoming for their construction. The present economic recession has exacerbated the problem, and it is clear that neither donors nor governments are willing or able to invest large sums in new construction as opposed to reconstruction and

---

* references in the text are given at the back of the book

rehabilitation. Equally it would seem that previous investment strategies vis-à-vis transport have not been as successful as it was assumed. In particular, recent research [2, 3, 4] has drawn attention to the fact that:

— Few regular transport services operate away from all-weather road networks. However, many people live remote from such networks, and hence lack access to transport services.
— In areas with all-weather road access, motor vehicles are beyond the financial means of the majority of people. Equally, many people cannot afford to use the transport services which do operate.

There is unlikely to be a significant improvement in this situation for the foreseeable future given the limited resources available for expansion of road networks and motor vehicle fleets, and the problems of maintaining existing roads [5, 6] and operating conventional motor vehicles.

It is perhaps the limitation of resources, rather than the dissatisfaction with previous policy, that has led to a consideration of alternative strategies. The use of labour-based techniques in road construction is just one example of the search for low-cost alternatives. One of the major barriers, however, to the formulation of alternative strategies is the paucity of knowledge of the transport needs of rural communities. Their transport needs are assumed to be taken into account within the overall framework of transport provision. The latter usually, however, relates to motorized vehicles on conventional roads.

This book has two related purposes:

1 to improve understanding of the nature of the transport needs of rural people in developing countries and of the extent, and means whereby, they are currently met;
2 to contribute to the development of practical policies to provide transport facilities which will better meet the needs of rural communities.

The core of the book is the series of case studies presented in Chapters 1-10. These cover nine developing countries in Africa, Asia and the Pacific. The studies encompass countries at different stages of development, from those at the most impoverished levels (Bangladesh and Tanzania) to those which have sizeable industrial and market economy sectors, and relatively high per capita incomes (Republic of Korea and Malaysia). They also cover a variety of different agricultural, social and geographic conditions and include a wide variety of different human, animal and motor-powered means of transport used to meet local movement needs.

The studies offer different perspectives on, and approaches to, the investigation of rural transport. The common, and distinctive, feature which links the case studies is that they examine rural transport conditions and problems from the viewpoint of rural people — small farmers, village households etc. They focus attention on the nature of small farmer and household transport needs, and on the physical and other constraints within which these must be satisfied. Much of the analysis is concerned with what the ILO has defined as the 'local transport system', that is the means whereby the majority of the rural population transport themselves, their families and their goods. A consequence of this focus is that the studies pay explicit attention to the role of simple, low-cost forms of transport and to the transport activities that take place remote from the motorable road network.

The studies [7] did not have a common research framework. They are therefore quite diverse in their coverage: from the analysis of transport needs in the Makete District of Tanzania to the description of one particular mode of transport, the *chee-geh*, in the Republic of Korea. They are all, however, illustrative of the local transport system.

The case studies have been grouped into three parts. The first comprises studies of the travel patterns of rural communities. The seond looks at particular means of local level transport. The studies that form the third part are more concerned with evaluations of transport policy and how it affects rural communities.

In editing the studies, every effort has been made to maintain the balance and perspective of the originals findings. Each study is prefaced by a short introduction to explain the focus and context of the original investigations. A brief assessment of the pertinent findings and implications is provided at the end of each study.

It would have been easy to prejudge the case studies by providing a detailed rationale for the study of the local transport system, but it is our view that the case studies are much more eloquent in providing such a rationale given their diversity and specificity. We have however attempted to draw together the most important lessons from the case studies in Chapter 11. This final chapter reviews the most important findings of the case studies, draws on supporting evidence from other sources revealed in the research associated with the production of this book and discusses the implications of these findings for the development of more effective policies for the planning and provision of local level rural transport facilities.

PART I — TRANSPORT PATTERNS

CHAPTER 1

Smallholder Transport Requirements in Malaysia[†]

Introduction

Peninsular Malaysia has a relatively high per capita income. In 1981, GNP stood at US$1,840, compared with US$770 for Thailand and US$790 for the Philippines. Income is not equally distributed, however, and the problems of the rural areas of Malaysia are not dissimilar to those of other countries in the region.

The study on which this chapter is based focused on the transport requirements of smallholder agriculture. It was commissioned by the ILO and carried out by J.D. Smith at the Kedah State Economic Planning Unit. It examined the transport requirements of a particular sub-district of the State and provided some ideas on the ways in which the demand could be met.

The study was carried out in 1981. National level data were drawn from existing official publications. Local level data were based on interviews with 184 households and on surveys of traders and other relevant groups, complemented by the findings of previous socio-economic surveys in the study area.

Background

Although per capita incomes are relatively high in Peninsular Malaysia the statistics show that in many rural areas the majority of the Malay population are living at or near the poverty line. The

---

[†]The study on which this chapter is based is described in J.D. Smith, 'Transport Technology and Employment in Rural Malaysia' (Geneva, ILO, 1981; mimeographed World Employment programme research working paper; restricted). Exchange rate at the time of the study M$2.38 (Malaysian dollars) = US$1.0.

Government's socio-economic policies aim to eradicate this poverty and redistribute incomes.

The sub-district of Jeneri in the State of Kedah was chosen for the detailed studies (Figure 1). Kedah has a population of about 1.1 million (the population of Peninsular Malaysia is 11,138,000 (1980 census)). Eighty-eight per cent of households in the State of

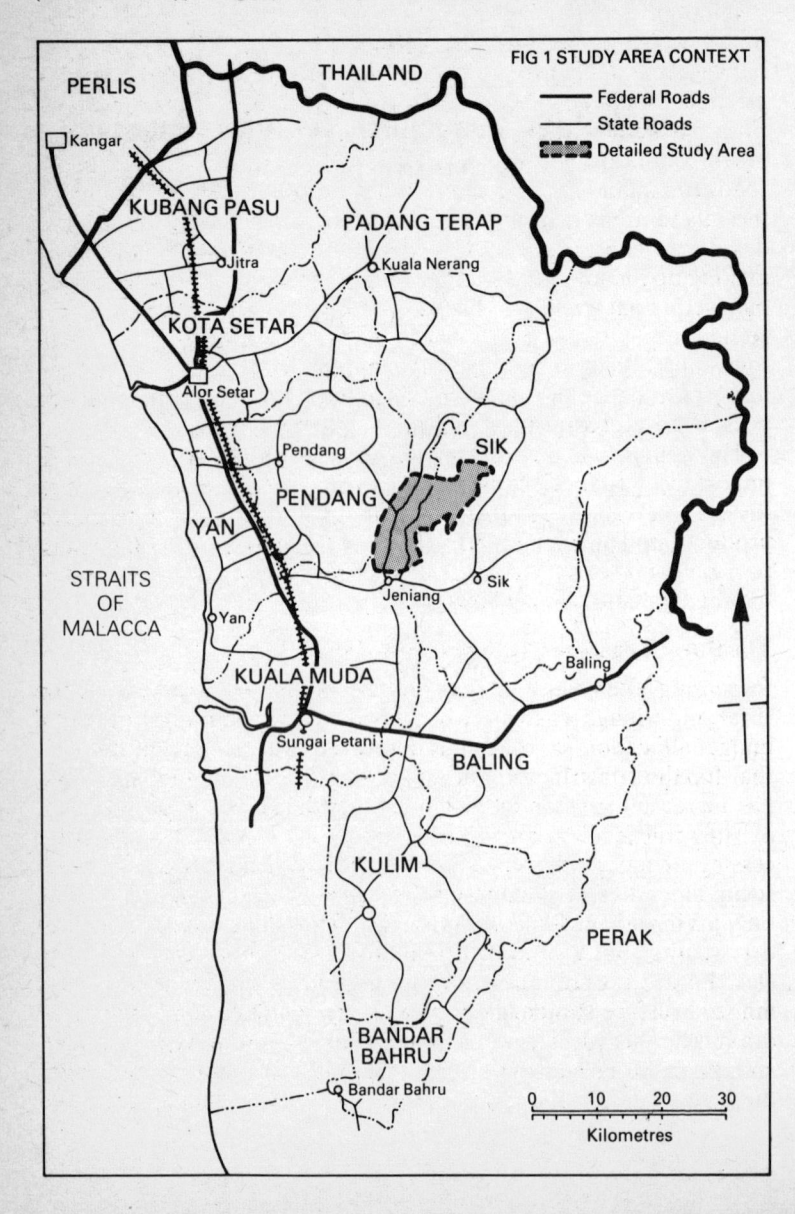

FIG 1 STUDY AREA CONTEXT

Kedah are in the rural areas and are principally engaged in agricultural activities, 59 per cent of households in the State are considered to be living at or near the poverty line. Jeneri is a poor agricultural area which is less well developed in terms of infrastructure than other areas in the State of Kedah and the peninsula. The population of 9,500 people depend upon farming for their livelihood. Jeneri (Figure 2) lies in the 'central belt' of Kedah State, which represents the greater part of the land area lying between the developed coastal plain in the west and the steep forest areas along the eastern boundary. The main road transport corridor in Kedah State is Federal Highway Route 1 which runs north-south through the coastal plain. From this Highway, several roads run inland to serve the rest of the State. The road network in the inland areas is oriented towards providing access to the more developed coastal plain. The standard and quality of the roads making up the inland network vary significantly depending on various factors but mostly on the state of development of the area concerned. Piped water supply is rare in the inland areas. Apart from some small isolated systems and some small-scale gravity feed systems installed by the Ministry of Health, most rural areas rely on wells and watercourses.

The main crops grown in the Jeneri study area are, in order of importance, rubber, padi (rice) and fruit. At the national level these three crops also represent the major share of agricultural production. This means that the study findings on the total transport demand related to these crops are certainly also relevant at the regional and peninsular level.

The Rural Transport System in Malaysia

Increasing emphasis is being placed on the development of the rural and village road network in Malaysia. Although the total budget allocation for roads has decreased over the period 1976-85, that for the construction and upgrading of rural and village roads has increased substantially. Under the village roads programme, existing tracks are being upgraded to facilitate marketing and processing of agricultural produce, and to provide better access to social amenities. Village roads are below official standards having only a 3 m wide unsurfaced pavement. They are passable by cars in dry weather but are more usually used by motorcycles and bicycles. Future programmes propose upgrading the roads to a bituminized surface standard on the existing alignment and improving drainage. This will allow all-weather use by motorcycles, bicycles and other simple vehicles. The low standard of construction makes these roads less suitable for pick-ups and lorries unlike the rural

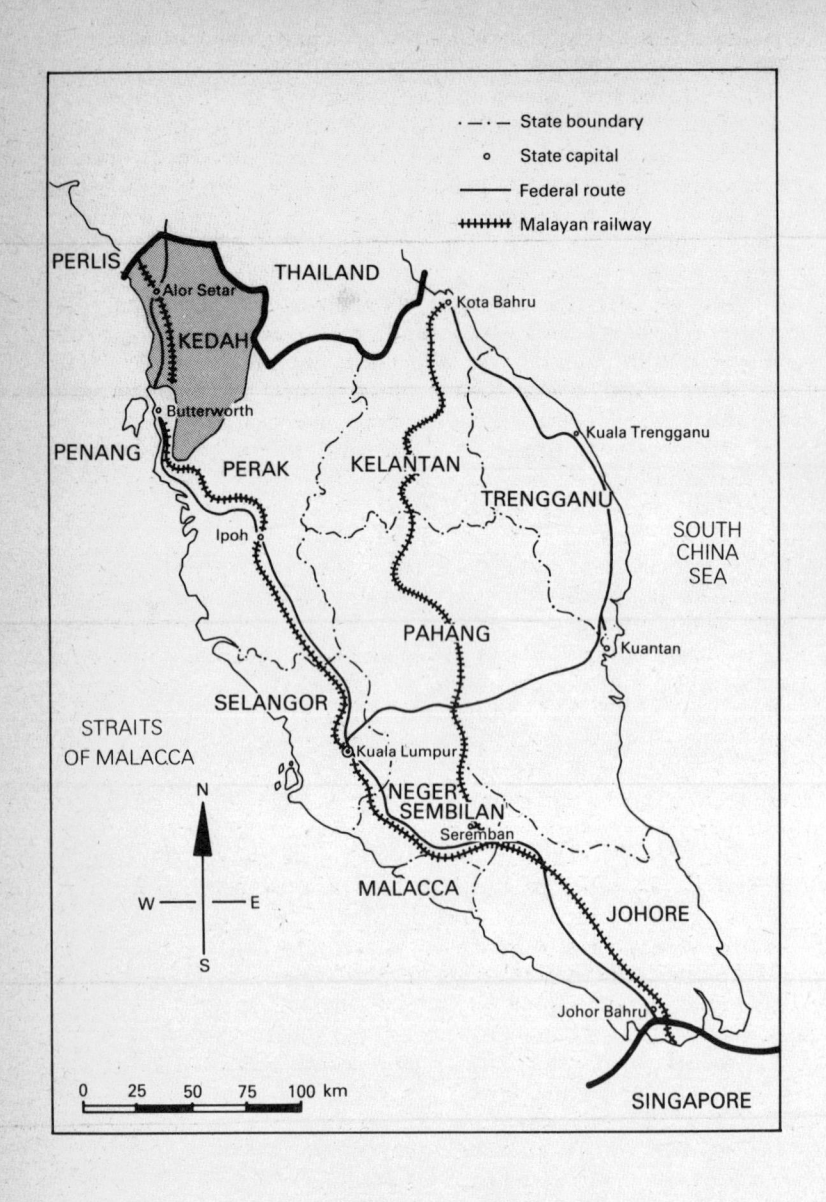

Fig. 2 *Kedah and the Study Area*

roads constructed by the Public Works Department. The latter are of a higher standard, in principle suitable for year-round use by heavy motorized transport.

Table 1 shows the distribution of vehicle ownership in Peninsular Malaysia.

The data indicate the relatively high level of motorization in Malaysia, and show the dominance of 'conventional' motor vehicles, in contrast to the locally developed modes (e.g. the jeepney) found in other Asian countries. They also indicate the limited range (bicycles and tricycles) of simple vehicles available for use by low-income households compared with other countries in the region.

Vehicle ownership and household income
Table 2 shows the level of vehicle ownership by households in the study area based on data from the sample interview survey.

Table 1. Peninsular Malaysia Road Transport

	No. of Vehicles	Vehicles per 100 population
Motorized:		
Cars	555,358	5.1
Motorcycles	1,079,020	9.9
Buses	11,589	0.1
Trucks and vans	122,543	1.1
Taxis	12,051	0.1
Others[1]	49,397	0.5
Sub-total	1,829,958	16.8
Non-motorized:		
Bicycles	1,416,000	13.0
Tricycles[2]	12,608	0.1
Sub-total	1,428,608	13.1
Total	3,258,566	29.9

[1] Includes tractors, road rollers and trailers.
[2] Excludes goods-carrying tricycles.

Table 2. Vehicle Ownership by Household

Households with	No.	%
No vehicle	24	13.1
Bicycle	58	31.5
Motorcycle	42	22.8
Motorcycle and bicycle	49	26.6
Car	4	2.2
Car and motorcycle	3	1.6
Car and motorcycle and bicycle	2	1.1
Boat	1	0.5
Truck/van	1	0.5
Total	184	99.9

The high levels of motorcycle and bicycle ownership are noteworthy. However car and truck ownership is very low in the study area, and is much less than the average for the peninsula.

Household income in the study area is also low. Eighty-nine per cent of the households had incomes lower than M$250 per month, as compared with the average monthly income of M$590 for rural households elsewhere in Peninsular Malaysia. Over 90 per cent of the households in the study area derive their income from the cultivation and sale of agricultural produce. The amount of disposable income is subject to considerable variation because of changes in commodity price levels and agricultural yields.

Other data collected during general household expenditure surveys indicate that between 12 and 16 per cent of monthly household incomes is expended on transport and communications. This means that approximately M$20 to 30 per month will be available for such things as fuel, bus and taxi fares, vehicle repairs or the purchase of new or second-hand vehicles. The survey data confirm this; only 20 per cent of households spent more than M$30 on transport.

A standard bicycle costs around M$160, the best-selling motorcycle — a 70 cc Japanese model — costs around M$1,650 and the best-selling car — a 1,200-1,300 cc Japanese model — costs about M$15,000, of which 35-40 per cent would be required as a deposit. For the majority of the population the cost of a new bicycle represents their total monthly household income or between 6-8 months of their average expenditure on transport. The purchase of a new motorcycle represents some 10 months total income or nearly 8 years of the average expenditure on transport for the poorest farmers. The M$5,250 deposit for a standard saloon car in the peninsula is clearly out of the range of study area households.

Given the prices of new bicycles and motorcycles, the fact that 60 per cent of the households own a bicycle and 50 per cent own a motorcycle suggests that the majority of purchases were of second-hand vehicles. Various types of informal credit or cash arrangements exist between smallholder and trader and facilitate the purchase of second-hand bicycles and motorcycles. The substantial increase in motorcycle ownership which has taken place over the period 1970-81 can be partly explained by the introduction of new loan schemes by rural credit institutions. The small percentage of car-owning households indicates that, in terms of financial outlay, a vast difference exists between the ownership of cars and motorcycles.

The level of bicycle and motorcycle ownership in the study area suggests that even the low disposable income available for transport is sufficient for the purchase of substantial numbers of (second-hand) bicycles and motorcycles. It also suggests that transport is high on the priority list of rural people with very low incomes and that they are prepared to spend a sizeable proportion of their monthly income to satisfy their movement needs.

Transport for agricultural purposes
The way in which the local population use the transport system is a function of a variety of factors including level of access, cropping patterns, vehicle ownership and the state of the network. In general, however, transport can be divided by location into on-farm and off-farm transport and by function into agricultural and other.

Ninety per cent of the households in the study area are smallholders, of whom 92 per cent grow rubber, 47 per cent padi and 18 per cent fruits. The significance of rubber to the smallholder lies in the fact that it is useful only as a cash crop and as such provides his main source of income. Padi and fruits are grown partly for home consumption.

Table 3 shows that nearly half of the smallholders in the study area have rubber as the only crop and that rubber and padi together account for nearly 80 per cent of the total cultivation.

Table 4 presents data on the on- and off-farm transport requirements for the major agricultural crops produced by smallholders in the study area. The table shows that transport requirements are related predominantly to the production of padi and rubber.

Inputs of fertilizer, seedlings and insecticides are generally provided free of charge by government agencies and are delivered once a year to the farm gate or a local collection point. The average trip lengths (14-20 km) and the total transport requirements per farm (227 kg for padi and 488 kg for rubber) are high. The significant difference between the two major crops is that inputs are used by most padi farmers but only by 25 per cent of rubber farmers.

In terms of transporting agricultural outputs, the requirements for padi and rubber are totally different. Two-thirds of the padi produced is for home consumption and is either processed at home or taken to the nearest rice mill. The average production of padi per farm is 1,285 kg. Padi is harvested once or twice per year and thus gives rise to a requirement for bulk transportation over fairly long distances.

In contrast, smallholders tap rubber for about 200 days per year. The rubber must be collected every one or two days and sold in the form of latex, scrap or sheets. Each type of rubber can be marketed through government agencies or private sector traders. The government agencies provide collection centres and processing services. The private sector competes with the Government by providing the same services with the added flexibility of farmgate collection. The smallholder has the option, based on price levels,

Table 3. Farming Patterns

	No. of smallholder farms	% Farms	Total area (ha)	% Total	Average Farm Size (ha)
Rubber only	911	48.3	1,430	19.0	1.6
Rubber and padi	536	28.4	1,287	17.1	2.4
Rubber, padi and fruits	215	11.4	630	8.4	2.9
Rubber and fruits	85	4.5	201	2.7	2.4
Padi only	96	5.1	99	1.3	1.0
Padi and fruits	43	2.3	48	0.6	1.1
Sub-total	1,886	100.0	3,695	49.1	2.0
Non-productive rubber	—	—	2,248	29.9	—
Other[1]	—	—	1,574	20.9	—
Total	—	—	7,517	100.0	—

[1] Includes non-productive fruits, other crops and rubber farmed by non-Jeneri smallholders (probably untitled squatters).

Table 4. Agricultural Transport Requirements by Commodity

Commodity	Quantity (% of total tonnage)	Off-farm Average trip length/km	Off-farm % of total tonne/km	On-farm Average trip length/km	On-farm % of total tonne/km
Inputs[1]					
Padi[2]	6.8	19.6	17.0	0.15	5.1
Rubber[3]	5.9	14.3	10.8	0.25	7.4
Outputs					
Padi home	27.4	6.8	23.9	0.15	20.6
Padi sale	13.0	18.2	30.2	0.15	9.7
Rubber scrap[4]	38.9	3.1	15.5	0.25	48.8
Rubber sheets	2.2	3.1	0.9	0.25	2.7
Rubber latex	2.6	3.1	1.0	0.25	3.3
Fruits home	1.7	1.8	0.4	0.15	1.1
Fruits sale	1.5	1.8	0.3	0.15	1.1
Total	100.0	—	100.0	—	100.0

[1] Fruits inputs insignificant.
[2] Over 70% of padi farmers use all inputs and 97% fertilizer.
[3] Less than 27% of rubber farmers use any inputs.
[4] All rubber is sold.
[5] Trip length weighted for destinations west and east of River Muda.
Source: Study estimates based on survey data.

of using any purchasing agency for his produce. Thus the main transport need of the smallholders for rubber products is short-distance transport of relatively small quantities from farm to group collection centre.

Table 5 details the modes used for off-farm transport of inputs and outputs. Because they involve bulk transportation over fairly long distances, the movement of inputs is predominantly by truck (78 per cent) and motorcycle (12 per cent). Similarly, marketed padi is transported mainly by truck (70 per cent) and motorcycle (25 per cent). However for movement over shorter distances, the pattern changes. Transport of rubber (from farm gate to first level buyer/dealer) is by motorcycle (60 per cent) and bicycle (25 per cent), and of padi for home consumption by motorcycle (50 per cent), truck (23 per cent), car/taxi (14 per cent) and bicycle (13 per cent). Overall, motorcycles account for 42 per cent of transport of agricultural outputs, trucks 38 per cent and bicycles 13 per cent.

The generally small size of holdings means that on-farm movements are short-ranging as Table 4 shows, from about 0.15 to 0.25 km on average. It has been estimated that on-farm movements amount to only 2.5 per cent of the total tonne/km. However, over 90 per cent of agricultural inputs and outputs (a total of 3,750 tonnes in the study area) are moved on the farm by human porterage. Various methods of head, shoulder and backloading are used, but shoulder poles and yokes are by far the most common. In addition to movement on the farm, transport is also required to travel to and from the smallholding. As Table 6 shows, these journeys are made predominantly on foot and by bicycle. (Note: In this case-study the term 'on-farm transport' is used to refer specifically to movement on the farm land itself. In the remainder of the

Table 6. Mode of Transport to Smallholding by Farm Type (%)

Mode	Rubber	Padi	Fruits
Walk	56.7	73.6	90.6
Bicycle	31.1	20.9	9.4
Motorcycle	10.4	5.5	—
Car/Taxi	1.8	—	—
Total	100.0	100.0	100.0

Table 5. Summary of Off-farm Vehicle Use in the Study Area

Commodity (tonne/km)	Walk	Bicycle	Motor cycle	Truck	Car/Taxi	Total	%
Inputs[1]							
Padi[2]	174	133	294	4,138	223	4,963	17.0
Rubber	—	146	600	2,274	152	3,172	10.8
Outputs							
Padi home	—	902	3,494	1,579	1,013	6,988	23.9
Padi sale	—	442	2,212	6,193	—	8,847	30.2
Rubber sale	188	1,332	3,182	320	61	5,084	17.4
Fruits home	105	11	—	—	—	116	0.4
Fruits sale	14	10	73	5	—	106	0.3
Sub-total	481	2,977	9,855	14,509	1,449	29,272	100.0
% of Total	1.6	10.2	33.7	49.6	4.9	100.0	

[1] Inputs transported by modes other than truck represent mainly private sector purchases.

book it is used in a broader sense to refer to movement in and around the village, between village and farm, and on the farm.)

Transport for non-agricultural purposes
Information from the household interviews indicates that significant numbers of passenger trips are made to schools, shops and medical facilities, and for services and repairs. The most important of these, in that they are carried out on a regular daily basis, are trips to school and sundry shopping. Visits to coffee shops, local clinics and fruit and vegetable markets are also significant on a weekly basis. Table 7 gives details of these trips by mode of travel.

For daily trips to school and to the shops, walking is by far the most important mode of transport. Bicycle trips to secondary schools, sundry shops and coffee shops are also important. The latter two will usually be made in non-farmwork time. Secondary and, to a lesser extent, primary school trips would conflict with work trips if school attendance is required during the morning shift in households owning only one bicycle. The proportion of bicycle trips reflects the relatively short average trip lengths and small goods-carrying requirements (from sundry shops) for these purposes. In contrast the heavy use of the local bus system for weekly clinic and market trips, mainly by females, and children's school trips reflects longer average trip lengths, the non-availability of bicycles and motorcycles, the inability to drive motorcycles and the larger carrying capacity requirements for weekly shopping or marketing.

Provision of transport
The study revealed that for on-farm transport human porterage is ubiquitous. The shoulder pole, which is the most common method

Table 7. Daily and Weekly Non-agricultural Trips by Mode (%)

Trip	Walk	Bicycle	Motor cycle	Car/ Taxi	Bus	Total
Daily						
School Primary	60.8	8.8	5.7	2.1	22.6	100.0
School Secondary	38.5	21.1	0.9	—	39.5	100.0
Sundry shop	47.8	18.5	25.8	3.4	4.5	100.0
Weekly						
Coffee shop	18.9	17.6	43.2	8.1	12.2	100.0
Clinic	4.7	4.7	13.6	35.5	41.5	100.0
Market	0.6	2.8	18.6	35.1	42.9	100.0

used, has a long history in Malaysia. Even though increased rural income has engendered a move towards the use of bicycles and motorcycles, the shoulder pole remains an important aid to on-farm transport and almost every smallholder possesses one or more. Whilst the shoulder pole looks simple (Plate 1) it is, in fact, an ingenious device. The pole is flexible and is designed to move in harmony with the carrier. The pole is used to transport small loads (up to 50 kg) over short distances (up to about 1 km), and has the advantage that it can be used over rough ground. Shoulder poles are usually made from hardwood or bamboo and fashioned at home at no cost.

In the study area, 13 per cent of households own no vehicle at all and a further 31.5 per cent only a bicycle. The bicycle therefore is for many the only means of transport and what others aspire to. The bicycle is of significant importance for rural transport of goods and passengers, being used for travel to smallholdings, for the movement of crops and for non-agricultural trips. It is a multi-functional vehicle that can be used by different members of the household. Hitherto only few modifications, notably the fitting of a rear carrier, have been made to the standard design to increase its useful carrying capacity. However, potential may exist for improvements to the goods-carrying capacity of bicycles which could generate additional local employment. The urban location and large size of the major bicycle manufacturers indicates that potential markets for any improved goods-carrying bicycle or tricycle would have to be large to warrant their attention. In contrast, the local adaptation or modification of standard designs to suit individual crop and yield requirements could prove sufficiently profitable to warrant the establishment of small-scale workshops and repair facilities.

The motorcycle is the major locally owned mode of off-farm transport. It would seem logical to concentrate efforts on the improvement or adaptation of the motorcycle to conform to transport needs. Presently much of the rubber, having been transported to the collection point on shoulder poles is transferred to the motorcycle (Plate 2). It would be sensible to consider the introduction of locally manufactured motorcycle trailers to provide a more effective means of transporting the rubber.

The conclusions of a survey on the existing levels of employment in the transport sector are of interest. At the national level, there is a general trend away from agricultural employment into manufacturing and other secondary and tertiary jobs. In the transport sector, this is reflected in the increase of the number of workers employed in the manufacture and assembly of bicycles, trishaws and tricycles by about 480 per cent over the period 1968-80. In 1980, employment in the manufacture and assembly of non-motorized vehicles made up over 11 per cent of total employment in the manufacture of transport equipment, compared to 8 per cent in 1968. It is estimated that non-motorized transport activities provide employment to as many as 25,000 people.

These figures show the growing importance of the sector in terms of employment creation: they also indicate that the requisite expertise is available to meet the demands of an expanded market. However, the geographical distribution of existing firms suggests that future manufacturing of non-motorized vehicles on a medium to large-scale will continue to be concentrated in the urban areas rather than in rural areas. Indeed, according to the 1973 Census there were only four firms employing a total of 42 workers in the manufacture of all types of transport equipment in Kedah as a whole. Small-scale assembly of vehicles can, on the other hand, be carried out in rural areas (as at present) but will usually be done in conjunction with the sale and repair of bicycles spare parts and accessories.

Support for the entrepreneurial sector

Given the potential demand for bicycles and motorcycles adapted to carry freight, and the fact that local people will spend a considerable proportion of their income on transport, it is worth examining the prospects of government support for the local manufacture of such vehicles.

There is significant government commitment to develop the entrepreneurial sector. The Government provides financial assistance to Malay entreprenuers in the form of low interest charges or high loan ceilings. Official government loans for small-scale activities can be obtained by smallholders using land titles as collateral. Loans can also be obtained through commercial banks, specialized industrialized finance institutions, rural credit institutions and the informal lending sector, including pawnshops.

In line with government policies, substantial portions of commercial bank and finance company lending are allocated to small-scale enterprise development including manufacturing and vehicle repair. However, since there are few commercial banks located outside the major urban centres their services are not readily accessible to the majority of smallholders. The fact that commercial banks prefer to limit their risks by providing low risk, high value loans makes them less accessible to the small-scale manufacturers.

The specialized industrial finance institutions are mainly geared to the financing of medium and large-scale industrial enterprises. Apart from the formal channels of credit, Malaysia has a system of pawnshops operated by private businessmen but licensed by individual states. The main advantages of pawnshops to small industrialists are their proximity to the grass-roots level of operation, their informality, particularly in terms of collateral requirements and their speed of transaction; the main drawback lies in the high interest rates.

Two other institutions provide loans or facilities to farmers and entrepreneurs, the Government Development Agencies and rural credit institutions. The latter are undoubtedly the most important source of funding available to smaller farm units such as those found in the study area. Unfortunately, however, in terms of the manufacture, assembly and repair of transport equipment the rural credit institutions have little or no commercial experience or expertise.

A survey of bicycle manufacturers and vehicle repair shops in the study area was carried out to define the difficulties they faced. Finance was only one of the problems identified by manufacturers and certainly not the most important. The supply of raw materials, spare parts and other inputs, and the fluctuating level of demand were identified as more important constraints to the development of the sector. The survey revealed that the majority of transport equipment and related businesses in this area are small family concerns providing mainly repair services to local inhabitants. Most of the Malay traders in this sector did not seem to be operating on a viable basis, and depended on agricultural activities to supplement their incomes.

Summary

Although income levels are low in the study area, smallholders are prepared to spend a considerable proportion of their income on transportation. Since the long distance transport of agricultural inputs and outputs is well-organized and reasonably available, the greatest demand would seem to be for on-farm and short distance off-farm transport of agricultural inputs and produce, and for personal transport. At present the bicycle and motorcycle are used for both these purposes and are within the financial reach of the majority of households, even in the low-income study area.

Head and shoulder loading remain dominant for on-farm transport. Considering the multi-purpose use of the bicycle and motorcycle, the greatest potential for improvements appears to be in increasing the goods-carrying capacity of these vehicles. The local adaption or modification of standard designs could prove sufficiently rewarding to guarantee the successful establishment of small-scale workshops and repair facilities in the rural areas. However, a number of constraints would need to be overcome before such developments could take place. Access to credit would need to be facilitated, and supplies (e.g. raw materials) would need to be readily available at reasonable cost. Furthermore, training in small enterprise management skills would be required to teach the entrepreneur the basics of organizing and administering his business. Most important, however, would be to identify which types of modifications/improvements would be most useful and to examine the commercial viability of satisfying this demand at the local level.

CHAPTER 2

Rural Transport in India[†]

Introduction

The bullock cart is one of the major means of transport in India. It is estimated that there are some 15 million carts of which 12 million are in the rural areas[1].

In 1977, the Indian Ministry of Shipping and Transport sponsored a nationwide socio-economic study of animal cart transport. The objective of the survey was to obtain a better understanding of the role and usage of animal carts in rural areas. Separate surveys were carried out in the northern and southern regions of India. The northern region survey, carried out by the National Council of Applied Economic Research (NCAER), covers rural areas in seven Indian States accounting for nearly 50 per cent of the country's rural population. There are estimated to be over 6 million animal carts in use in the region covered by the survey. Data was gathered in 1977-78 by direct interviews with a stratified sample of 1,150 households and 200 cart manufacturers and repairers.

This case study is based on the findings of that survey, and a supplementary survey of 200 households and 30 cart manufacturers carried out in 1980. Data on employment aspects of rural transportation are drawn from separate studies carried out previously by NCAER.

Background

There is a wide spectrum of transport modes in India, ranging from trains and motorized vehicles through many different types

---

[†]The study on which this chapter is based is described in the National Council of Applied Economic Research, *Transport Technology for the Rural Areas: India*, (Geneva, ILO, July 1981; mimeographed World Employment Programme research working paper; restricted). Exchange rate at time of study 9.7 Rupees = US$1.0.

Table 8. Road Access to Villages

Population category	Total number of villages	Connected with all weather road	Connected with fair weather road	Not connected with any road
1,500 and above	69,681	37,729	13,949	18,003
1,000-1,500	54,623	22,985	9,816	21,822
Less than 1,000	451,632	107,925	69,062	274,645
Total	575,936	168,639	92,827	314,470

of animal- and human-powered devices to headloading. Motorized vehicles have only recently begun to play a role in rural transportation. This role is at present a minor one and is unlikely to become more significant in the near future. A major reason for this is the low standard and relatively poor condition of the rural road network. Table 8 details the status of the Indian rural road network in March 1978. In this instance 'connected' was defined as being not more than 1.6 km from the road.

Thus 55 per cent of villages have no road access and a further 16 per cent have only a low-standard, fair-weather road connection. The surveys also showed that approximately 75 per cent of all rural goods transport takes place on unsurfaced roads. Another 12 per cent takes place on roads which are only partly surfaced. There is little doubt that this situation will remain as such for a long time to come, as resources for road improvement and maintenance are limited and are unlikely to increase in real terms.[2]

Another important factor limiting the use of motorized vehicles in rural areas is the nature of the transport needs of the majority of the people. The surveys established that about 90 per cent of rural goods traffic relates to the movement of farm inputs, products and equipment. The transport of foodgrains, sugar cane and food accounts for 65 per cent, commercial crops for 8 per cent, and farm inputs, of which manure is the most important, for 16 per cent. The remaining 11 per cent of rural goods traffic relates to the transport of construction materials such as bricks, mud, tinsheets, etc., and fuels such as firewood and dung cakes. Fodder and manure account for two-thirds of the goods transported within the village boundaries. The major goods moved outside the villages are commercial crops and vegetables. The surveys also showed

Table 9. Transportation of Goods in Rural Areas

	Quantity (million tonnes)	Tonne-km (million)	Average trip distance (km)
Within village	520	842	1.5
Outside village	124	1,064	8.3
Total	644	1,905	1.9

that transport by the household sector dominates rural goods traffic. The household sector accounts for over 80 per cent of rural goods movements in terms of tonne-km, and approximately 95 per cent of the total quantity of goods moved in rural areas. The remainder is transported by commercial establishments and the rural industrial sector. Table 9 shows the quantities moved and average distance of trips made within and outside the village boundaries. This suggests that for agriculture, transport needs are primarily for the movement of small quantities of goods over relatively short distances. The average distance over which goods are transported is approximately 1.9 km. In terms of weight of goods, about 81 per cent are transported within the village limits.

Requirements for longer distance transport are less frequent, at irregular intervals, and often relate to travel for social purposes. It is not surprising therefore that tractors and buses are the only types of motorized vehicles which have had a significant impact on rural transportation. Tractors are within the financial reach of the wealthier people in rural areas and are utilized for a multitude of purposes, of which transport is only one. Buses provide relatively cheap services which cater for the longer distance transport needs of rural people.

By far the most important mode of rural transport in India is the animal cart. Table 10 shows that, in terms of tonne-km, animal carts account for over 68 per cent of the goods traffic in the rural areas. In terms of tonnes moved, they handle 72 per cent of the goods. The comparatively large share of goods handled by headloading and the importance of this mode of transport for shorter trips is also worth noting. However, headloading is used predominantly within the village, while animal carts account for 65 per cent of goods traffic outside the village as well as 72 per cent within. Because animal carts are slow, motorized modes become the most

Table 10. Transportation of Goods by Mode of Transport

Mode of transport	Average trip distance (km)	million tonnes	% share	million tonne/km	% share
Headloading	1.5	113	17.7	170	9.0
Bicycle, tricycle	4.5	4	0.5	10	0.6
Pack animals	1.0	2	0.3	2	0.1
Animal carts	2.6	462	71.8	1,307	68.6
Tractor-trailer	5.4	59	9.3	353	18.5
Truck, light commercial vehicle	18.5	4	0.5	64	3.3
All modes	1.9	644	100.0	1,906	100.0

important means of transport for trip distances above 10 km. Tractor-trailer combinations play a significant role for medium-distance trips and account for 7.5 per cent of transport within villages. Trucks are important for long-distance trips but account for only 0.5 per cent of the total quantity of goods transported.

Ownership patterns

Table 11 shows the distribution of vehicle ownership by income group.

Seventy-four per cent of rural households do not own any vehicle. Ninety per cent of these households have incomes of less than Rs6,000 per annum and only 1.5 per cent belong to income groups above Rs12,000. The major reason given for not acquiring a vehicle is simply lack of finance. However, about 30 per cent of the households indicated that they did not need a vehicle, mainly because their landholdings were very small. A very small proportion of the households, 0.2 per cent, indicated that the lack of roads in their area was the reason for not owning transport.

Animal carts are the dominant type of transport, being owned by 17 per cent of the total number of households and used by approximately 48 per cent. Most of the non-owners borrowed the

Plate 1 *A shoulder pole used by a fish farmer in Indonesia*

Plate 2 *A motor-cycle being used to carry rubber in Malaysia*

Plate 3 *A modern cart with pneumatic tyres and roller bearings*

Plate 4 *Traditional wooden-wheeled cart drawn by a pair of bullocks*

Table 11. Per cent Share of Households Owning Different Vehicles or Using Animal Carts in Different Income Classes

Household income group (Rs.)	Percentage of households in income group owning				Households not owning any vehicles (%)	Users of animal carts (%)
	Animal carts	Tractors	Buses	Bicycles		
Up to 3,000	4.1	—	—	13.1	83.7	39.6
3,001 - 6,000	12.6	—	—	6.9	81.7	41.1
6,001 - 9,000	51.7	4.0	—	8.2	38.0	82.1
9,001 - 12,000	43.7	1.1	6.9	5.4	46.3	65.3
12,001 - 15,000	60.3	5.1	—	1.3	31.5	80.0
Over 15,000	51.4	17.3	—	5.6	31.4	76.7
Total	16.8	0.9	0.4	9.2	74.0	41.6

Note: Aggregate percentages in any income group may exceed 100 as a household may own more than one type of vehicle.

Table 12. Percentage Share of Households Owning Different Vehicles by Operational Holding

Operational holding (hectares)	Animal carts	Tractors	Buses	Bicycles	Not owning any vehicle
Up to 2.0	3.8	—	—	6.1	91.1
2.1- 5.0	36.0	—	—	16.9	49.0
5.1-10.0	41.6	1.9	0.1	14.3	43.9
Over 10.0	45.0	12.2	6.5	7.6	31.7
Total	16.8	0.9	0.4	9.2	74.0

carts from their friends or relatives without paying any charge. Some 10 per cent of the owners reported charging for hiring out carts. Tractors were not owned by households having an income below Rs6,000 per year and the proportion of tractor-owning households increased sharply at higher income levels.

Ownership of vehicles, with the exception of bicycles, is closely related to the size of landholding—as Table 12 shows.

Characteristics of animal cart use

Given the features of rural transportation in India, the popularity of animal carts is understandable. They can be used on sealed roads, rough tracks and cropland where a significant proportion of movement takes place during the harvest period. Animal power is abundant and cheaply available. The carts are produced and maintained with locally available skills and materials, and can carry a variety of loads ranging from manure to construction materials. Their average speed of 3-5 km per hour is adequate for the uses to which they are put and the distances travelled.

Table 13 shows the percentage distribution of numbers of trips and quantities transported categorized by trip distance. On average, animal carts make 265 trips per year with an average one-way trip distance of 2.58 km. About one trip in six is ouside the village. Eighty per cent of trips within the village are less than 2 km while over 60 per cent of trips outside the village are more than 5 km.

In general, the capacity of carts is under-utilized. On most trips the carts travel empty in one direction and the loads carried vary from a few kilograms to 2 tonnes. The carts are filled to capacity on about 19 per cent of trips and are less than half full on 46 per cent of trips. However, capacity utilization increases for trips outside the village when carts are fully loaded on 37 per cent of trips and less than half full on only 28 per cent.

Table 14 shows the intensity of cart use according to owners' income level. On average, carts are utilized for a total of 106 days per year, 73 days by the owner and 33 days on hire. Cart usage by the owner increases with income level. However, overall usage is highest at the extremes of income since the poorest owners hire or loan their carts for a substantial proportion of the time.

Animal carts provided an estimated total employment of 458.1 million man-days in Northern India in 1977-78. Ninety-three per cent of it emanated in the rural sector. Cart operation accounted for 90 per cent of the employment, the remainder being in manufacturing and repair. For India, as a whole, the employment due to animal carts is estimated to be in the region of 990 million workdays, and the rural component about 925 million work-days.

Types of animal carts

In Northern India, 78.0 per cent of animal carts are drawn by a pair of bullocks. The remainder are drawn by buffaloes (17.8 per cent), camels (3.8 per cent) and horses/ponies (0.6 per cent). Two different types of cart are widely used, the traditional variety with

Table 13. Percentage Share of Load Trips and Quantities Transported by Trip Distance

Trip distance (km)	Loaded cart trips Within village	Loaded cart trips Outside village	Loaded cart trips Total	Quantity transported Within village	Quantity transported Outside village	Quantity transported Total
Up to 0.5	10.0	0.3	8.6	10.2	0.2	8.1
0.6-1.0	41.3	2.6	35.4	41.7	2.4	33.5
1.1-2.0	34.5	5.6	30.2	34.0	7.4	28.5
2.1-3.0	9.5	11.4	9.8	9.4	8.8	9.3
3.1-5.0	3.1	17.8	5.3	2.8	22.9	7.0
5.1-7.5	1.2	18.5	3.8	1.1	24.6	6.0
7.6-10.0	0.2	22.5	3.6	0.4	18.0	4.0
10.1-15.0	0.1	11.8	1.8	0.1	9.1	2.0
15.1-20.0	neg.	5.9	0.9	neg.	3.2	0.7
Over 20.0	0.1	3.6	0.6	0.3	3.4	0.9
Total	100.0	100.0	100.0	100.0	100.0	100.0

large diameter wooden wheels and improved versions with pneumatic tyres and roller bearings (plates 3 and 4). About 24 per cent of the total number of carts are of the improved type.

The traditional carts have certain design deficiencies which result in strain and injury to draught animals, waste draught power and thus reduce carrying capacity, and cause damage to roads. The traditional yoke is inefficient and can cause injury to the animals, the carts are very heavy, the rough bush bearings have high frictional resistance and the narrow, often steel-rimmed wheels cut into road surfaces. The use of pneumatic tyres and roller bearings overcomes some of these disadvantages, allowing greater loads to be carried, eliminating road damage and providing greater comfort for passengers. However, the cost of the traditional cart is lower and, because of its wide availability, it is easy to acquire cheaply second-hand. A disadvantage of pneumatic tyres is that they are prone to punctures and repair and vulcanizing services are not readily available along rural roads.

There are a certain number of marked differences in the utilization of the two types of carts. Improved carts are more intensively used on surfaced roads where they carry 63 per cent of the goods transported. On lower standard roads the traditional carts are more common.

There are estimated to be over 80 million work animals, mostly bullocks, in India, of which about 25 million are used to pull carts. Animal power is cheap, and easy to obtain. As the data show, many animals are not used to haul carts and are therefore idle

Table 14. Intensity of Cart Use by Owners by Income Level

Income class (Rs. per annum)	Number of days a cart used		
	Self use	Hired use	Total
Up to 3,000	48	108	156
3,001 - 6,000	56	39	95
6,001 - 9,000	70	25	95
9,001 - 12,000	92	20	112
12,001 - 15,000	100	6	106
Over 15,000	129	3	132
Average	73	33	106

RURAL INDIA

Table 15. Annual Cart Costs (in Rupees)

	Improved cart	Traditional cart
Cost of cart	2,000	1,000
Annual maintenance cost[1]	121	56
Interest on capital (10%)	200	100
Depreciation[2]	125	66
Total annual cost	446	222

[1] Based on survey data.
[2] Based on cart-life of 16 years reported in survey.

when not used for agricultural purposes. Generally, when animals are used to pull carts it is in addition to their usage in agriculture. It is therefore reasonable to assume that their utilization for transportation is at marginal or zero cost. Table 15 details the annual costs for owning and operating animal carts assuming that the owner already has work animals for agricultural purposes which can be used for transportation at zero cost.

An average cart transports 72 tonnes of goods per year. Transport charges for animal carts vary between Rs2.5-3.0 per 100 kg for a fixed distance between the village and the nearest commercial centre. This gives imputed earnings of Rs1,800-2,160. This indi-

Table 16. Percent Share of Households Owning Carts of Different Values by Income Level

Income class (Rs)	Value of carts (Rs.) Up to 750	751 to 1,250	1,251 to 1,750	Over 1,750	All carts
Up to 3,000	60.1	32.0	6.4	1.5	100.0
3,001- 6,000	45.5	36.5	12.2	5.7	100.0
6,001- 9,000	60.5	15.9	15.1	8.4	100.0
9,001-12,000	56.9	20.5	12.7	9.9	100.0
12,001-15,000	51.5	15.9	18.6	14.0	100.0
Over 15,000	32.0	14.5	29.4	24.1	100.0
Total	53.1	24.3	14.1	8.5	100.0

cates that cart operation is economical given that annual costs range between Rs.222-446 depending on type of cart. However, the economics to the individual owner depend on the utilization of the cart, his ability to make the initial investment, the number of days the cart is hired out and on what basis, and the realistic value that should be assumed for his time when operating the cart for his own purposes.

Table 16 shows that the cheapest carts are most in demand and indicates a positive relationship between the income of the households and the value of the carts owned by them.

Finance for the manufacture and purchase of carts
The Government of India actively supports the development of small-scale rural and cottage industrial units. Such units generate employment, have low capital-intensity and are an effective mechanism for mobilizing resources and skills. It is the Government's policy to reserve the manufacture of over 800 different items, including animal carts to the small-scale sector. Small-scale industry development programmes are carried out by the State Governments. The services provided under such programmes include infrastructural works, technical guidance, training facilities and financial assistance.

The major part of these services is provided directly to small-scale entrepreneurs, of which cart manufacturing and repair units represent a considerable proportion. However, some agencies also provide credit facilities to farmers and agricultural labourers for the purchase of animal carts. Such financial support to the customers of the cart manufacturers greatly facilitates the sales of their products. Under the rules of these agencies the purchase price of the animal carts is remitted directly to the dealer or manufacturer on behalf of the borrower. Certain development programmes provide 25-50 per cent subsidies to small farmers and agricultural labourers for the purchase of animal carts.

There are five major sources of finance for small industrial units: state financial corporations, commercial banks, co-operative banks and societies, District Industries Centres and the 'Khadi and Village Industries Commission'. These institutions provide loans for the purchase of land, buildings, plant and machinery at favourable rates of interest. The amounts advanced and the period of repayment generally depend on the type of manufacturing activity. Various schemes provide for advantageous rates of interest to the educated unemployed and potential entrepreneurs with technical qualifications. Enterprises set up in backward districts usually qualify for lower than normal rates of interest. The Lead Bank

Scheme, which operates in all districts of the country, is of interest. In each district a designated bank, the 'Lead Bank' is given special responsibility for overall economic development. It prepares the credit plan for the district and, with the co-operation of other banks, financial institutions and government agencies, provides loans to different categories of borrowers. In many districts, the lead banks have provided finance to carpentry units (who often include cart manufacture among their activities) and to prospective buyers of pneumatic-tyred animal-drawn carts.

The co-operative banks provide one-year loans to artisans for working capital through primary co-operative societies. The loans are usually granted on the basis of promissory notes and securities from the members. For larger amounts these securities are supplemented by using goods as collateral. The loan applications are scrutinized and approved by a committee of government bank and primary society representatives.

In some states, the co-operative banks provide loans for the purchase of carts and animals. The terms vary from place to place. In one state, the borrower has to create a statutory charge on his land in favour of the primary society if he wants a loan for more than Rs1,000. In others the hypothecation of the cart itself in favour of the primary society is sufficient provided the borrower takes out an insurance policy for the cost of the cart, meets at least 15 per cent of the loan from his own resources, and purchases share capital of the co-operative to the equivalent of 10 per cent of the outstanding loan. The purchase price of the cart is remitted directly to the cart dealer or manufacturer.

During the household survey, 38 banks located near the study areas were interviewed about their policies towards the credit needs of cart manufacturers. Most of the banks provide loans to a maximum credit limit of Rs5,000 on the basis of personal securities. Only a small percentage of the banks resort to the hypothecation of the equipment concerned or to mortgaging fixed assets. The interest rates charged vary generally between 9 and 12 per cent, although cheaper rates (as low as 4 per cent) are available under special schemes.

During the surveys 251 cart manufacturing and repairing units were interviewed. Information was requested on the amount of capital invested, production, labour employed and the problems faced by the units. Over 80 per cent of these units had invested less than Rs5,000 in their business. The investments of the cart repairing units are comparatively smaller, the great majority being less than Rs2,000. Of the 251 units only 17 per cent had borrowed money during the year preceding the survey. Eight of these had borrowed from moneylenders, even though they charge interest rates ranging between 10 and 60 per cent. The second important source of loans is from banks, but the amounts borrowed are higher (averaging Rs3,720), compared with Rs1,710 from money lenders. Friends and colleagues are another source of capital, providing some 13 per cent of the total loan amount at interest rates ranging between 15 and 24 per cent.

Analysis of the problems faced by cart manufacturers and repairers showed financial difficulties, especially in relation to obtaining loans, to be the major problem. Second in importance is a lack of demand for animal carts. Further problems are the high prices and often the non-availability of raw materials and components. Apparently the relative abundance of credit schemes offering funds at reasonable rates does not result in credit being easily accessible to animal-cart manufacturing or repairing units.

The major obstacle in participating in government-backed credit schemes appears to be the lengthy and bureaucratic approach of the financial institutions responsible. In some cases, the procedures take up to a year to complete. The potential borrowers often have to obtain a large number of certificates from different agencies, especially when they do not have enough land, property or other personal securities to offer as collateral for their loans.

Various units complained about the indifferent attitude, and sometimes corruption, of officials dealing with loan requests. Some potential borrowers are harrassed instead of aided in securing their loans. These problems would appear to be due in large part to the fact that such officials are not well-motivated because they do not stand to gain anything personally. This results in well-intended government policies being effectively thwarted by defective implementation.

These factors force may enterprises, especially the smaller ones, to forgo the loan altogether or to turn to private sources, which means paying higher charges. Furthermore, a large number of self-employed persons or small enterprises are unable to obtain financial assistance as they are not in a position to provide the required down-payments or third party guarantees. Even in those cases when the entrepreneur qualifies for a loan, the time-consuming procedures often cause long delays which could defeat the objective for which the loan was originally required.

Summary

The animal cart is the major means of goods transportation in rural India and, given the limited extent and slow growth of the surfaced road network, is likely to remain important for a long time to come. However, the survey shows that household income is the main determinant of animal cart ownership. Seventy-four per cent of rural households do not own any type of vehicle, in most cases because they cannot afford one.

As part of the survey the concept of communal use of carts was presented as a means of extending access to those who cannot afford individual ownership. However, the reaction to this idea was generally indifference or scepticism. There is considerable potential for increasing the efficiency of animal carts since the traditional types have certain technical deficiencies. However, the link between income and cart ownership suggests that design improvements which increase cost would not be acceptable to the majority of the rural population. Given the low level of ownership of carts the survey suggests that greater emphasis should be placed on providing some form of transport to the majority rather than improving the existing modes.

There is no lack of schemes to provide finance at economical rates of interest for the manufacture and purchase of carts. However, the cumbersome and lengthy procedures and the requirements for securing loans make them inaccessible to many artisans and potential cart purchasers.

CHAPTER 3

Rural Transport in Northern Nigeria[†]

Introduction

Over the past decade and a half Nigeria has embarked on a wide range of major infrastructure investments with the aid of its oil revenues. Between 1972 and 1980 the length of paved road in the country increased by 60 per cent. At 13 km per 100 sq km, it has one of the highest road densities in Africa.

The study on which this chapter is based examined the transport demands of the rural population in one area of Northern Nigeria and the way in which these demands were met. It also attempted to evaluate the likely response of farmers to improvements in transport.

The study was in the form of a questionnaire to a sample of households in four groups during two separate periods of the year. It was carried out in 1981 by Dr. O. Adebisi of the University of Zaria.

Background

The area selected for the study was Borno State in the north-east of the country (Figure 3). It is among the least industrially developed parts of Nigeria, but is in the savannah region which extends over more than half the country and provides good agricultural conditions. Farming practices and general living conditions are similar throughout the Savannah vegetation belt. The study was focussed on the town of Potiskum (estimated population 80,000) and covered an area within a radius of 60 km from this centre.

The bulk of Nigeria's agricultural products come from rural areas, but there are now some semi-urban dwellers who engage in

---

[†]The study on which this chapter is based is described in O. Adebisi: *Transport Technology for the Rural Areas: Nigeria*, World Employment Programme; (Geneva, ILO, 1982); (mimeographed World Employment Programme, research Working Paper; restricted). Exchange rate at the time of the study ₦ 0.69 (Naira) = US$1.0.

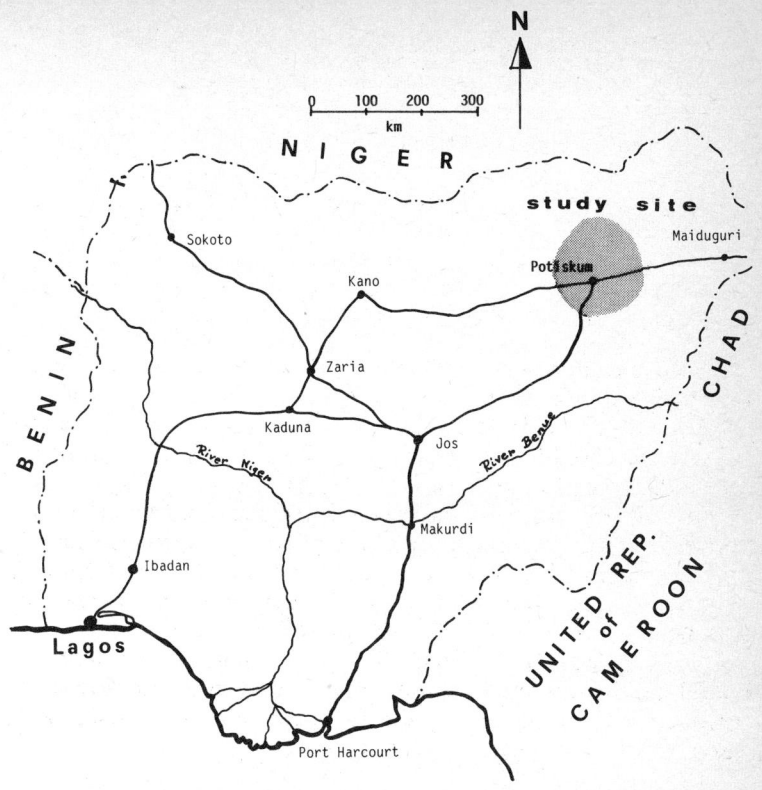

Fig. 3 *Map of Nigeria showing the study site*

farming. For the purposes of the study four types of farming household were defined on the basis of the size and accessibility of the settlements. Settlements were categorized as towns (population greater than 1,000), and villages (population less than 1,000). Accessibility was categorized as good—lying on an all-weather road—and poor—either linked by an unpaved road or not lying on an all-weather road. Settlements were selected for survey so that each of the four categories were approximately equally represented. In each settlement sample households were interviewed, the selection being made with the assistance of field agricultural officers to provide a representative cross-section of socio-economic characteristics. Two interview surveys were made, each with a sample size of 600, the two samples being selected independently. The first survey was carried out in July 1981 during the planting season, the second in October 1981 at the peak of harvesting. This approach reduced the number of questions asked of each household and hence enhanced the prospects of co-operation. Secondly, because questions asked at each stage were directly relevant to the prevailing transportation problems the data derived are likely to be more reliable than those depending upon recall.

Travel patterns of rural farmers

The following five categories of trip were found to be of direct relevance to the study:

1 trips to acquire farm inputs, including fertilizers, seedlings and farming implements;
2 trips to the farm;

Table 17. Travel Demand Characteristics of Farmers Resident in Villages not Lying on an All-weather Road

	Average number of annual person-trips/household				
Travel time (mins)	Trips for acquiring inputs	Trips to farms	Trips for domestic needs	Trips to markets	Recreational trips
0-5	15	31	22	17	—
5-10	9	418	116	41	1
10-15	8	500	41	17	—
15-20	10	365	13	39	2
20-25	15	—	30	20	1
25-30	5	608	77	28	3
30-60	8	365	18	44	3
60-120	—	—	—	—	3
120-180	—	—	—	—	2
Over 180	—	—	—	—	5
Total	70	2,787	317	206	20
Average travel time (mins)	18	18	17	21	80

3 trips to meet domestic needs — including those made to obtain firewood and construction materials;
4 trips to market to sell crops and to purchase food items;
5 recreational/social trips — including those made in order to participate in customary festivals and marriage celebrations.

In the study area the year consists of four main seasons:

1 the planting season (mid-June to end July);
2 the farming season (July to October);
3 the harvesting season (October to end of November);
4 the dry (off) season (December to June).

Trips to acquire farm inputs tend to be concentrated around the planting season. Trips to the farm are undertaken throughout the year but are more frequent during the farming and harvesting seasons. Domestic trips, except those to meet routine requirements, are concentrated during the off-season. Trips to the market to pur-

Table 18. Travel Demand Characteristics of Farmers Resident in Villages Lying on an All-weather Road

Average number of annual person-trips/household

Travel time (mins)	Trips for acquiring inputs	Trips to farms	Trips for domestic needs	Trips to markets	Recreational trips
0-5	1	898	72	—	—
5-10	2	939	55	20	1
10-15	2	565	172	26	—
15-20	1	423	189	1	—
20-25	1	—	13	2	—
25-30	2	—	1	30	2
30-60	5	—	—	4	7
Over 60	—	—	—	—	—
Total	14	2,825	502	83	10
Average travel time (mins)	25	8	13	19	41

chase food items are made mostly during the farming season while those to sell crops are during the harvesting and off-seasons. Recreational/social trips are normally made during the off-season.

Tables 17-20 give detailed breakdowns, for the four categories of farming households studied, of numbers of trips and travel times for different purposes. Table 21 summarizes the findings.

The average size of the households surveyed was about eight people which implies an average of 1.3 trips per person per day. In interpreting these findings it is important to note that some trips are undertaken for more than one purpose, e.g. a visit to the farm may be used as an opportunity to collect firewood.[1] Thus the breakdown of trip purposes is not precise. However, the results do show that, regardless of the accessibility and population of farmers' settlement, by far the most frequent trips are those to the

Table 19. Travel Demand Characteristics of Farmers Resident in Towns not Lying on an All-weather Road

Average number of annual person-trips/household

Travel time (mins)	Trips for acquiring inputs	Trips to farms	Trips for domestic needs	Trips to markets	Recreational trips
0-5	—	365	1	19	—
5-10	3	521	98	29	2
10-15	1	521	28	16	1
15-20	—	876	16	12	—
20-25	2	1,460	52	—	—
25-30	1	657	1	24	—
30-60	3	624	27	16	2
60-120	2	1,095	101	10	1
120-180	1	—	1	2	1
Over 180	—	—	—	—	1
Total	13	6,119	365	128	8
Average travel time (mins)	44	33	39	25	71

farm. Trips for domestic purposes and to markets come a distant second and third respectively. In terms of frequency, trips to acquire farming inputs are almost insignificant. However, the trips that do take place for this purpose are very important because these inputs constitute invaluable aids to successful farming.

Vehicle ownership patterns

Data on vehicle ownership were obtained from the survey households for the four types of vehicle encountered in the study area:

1 animals — mostly donkeys;
2 bicycles;
3 motorcycles;
4 motor vehicles — including passenger cars, pick-ups and mini-buses.

Table 20. Travel Demand Characteristics of Farmers Resident in Towns Lying on an All-weather Road

Travel time (mins)	Trips for acquiring inputs	Trips to farms	Trips for domestic needs	Trips to markets	Recreational trips
0- 5	6	—	5	39	—
5- 10	7	49	1	78	—
10. 15	7	106	104	63	24
15- 20	—	52	78	1	—
20- 25	—	140	—	—	—
25- 30	—	165	95	—	—
30- 60	—	160	159	—	—
60-120	—	185	146	—	2
120-180	—	161	94	—	1
Total	20	1,018	682	181	27
Average travel time (mins)	8	57	39	8	25

Table 21. Summary of Travel Demand Characteristics

	Farmers resident in			
	Villages remote from all-weather road	Villages on all-weather road	Towns remote from all-weather road	Towns on all-weather road
Average annual number of person-trips per household	3,411	3,433	6,632	1,926
Trips for different purposes as % of total trips				
— Inputs	2.1	0.4	0.2	1.1
— Farm	81.7	82.3	92.2	52.8
— Domestic	9.4	14.6	5.5	35.3
— Market	6.2	2.4	1.9	9.4
— Recreation	0.6	0.3	0.1	1.4

Data on vehicle ownership patterns are presented in Figure 4. There are on average:

1.0 donkey per household
0.9 bicycles per household
0.3 motorcycles per household
0.25 motor vehicles per household

However:

68.1 per cent of households have no animals
31.9 per cent of households have no bicycles
72.8 per cent of households have no motorcycles
84.5 per cent of households have no motor vehicles

Thus, although there are slightly more donkeys than bicycles, the latter is the most widely accessible vehicle with nearly 70 per cent of households owning at least one bicycle. Although donkeys occasionally serve individual households' needs for goods haulage they are, for the most part, hired out on a commercial basis. All households owning animals also own some other form of transport.

A good motorcycle costs about 8 times as much as a new bicycle, and a car in fairly good condition about 50 times as much. The relationship between vehicle ownership and household income has to be analyzed with care since some households own more than one vehicle type and/or operate vehicles commercially. Examin-

back view   side view

Plate 5 *Traditional Chee-geh*

Plate 6 *The Li-uh-Ka*

Plate 7 *The improved Chee-geh*

Plate 8 *A recently completed Jeepney awaiting delivery*

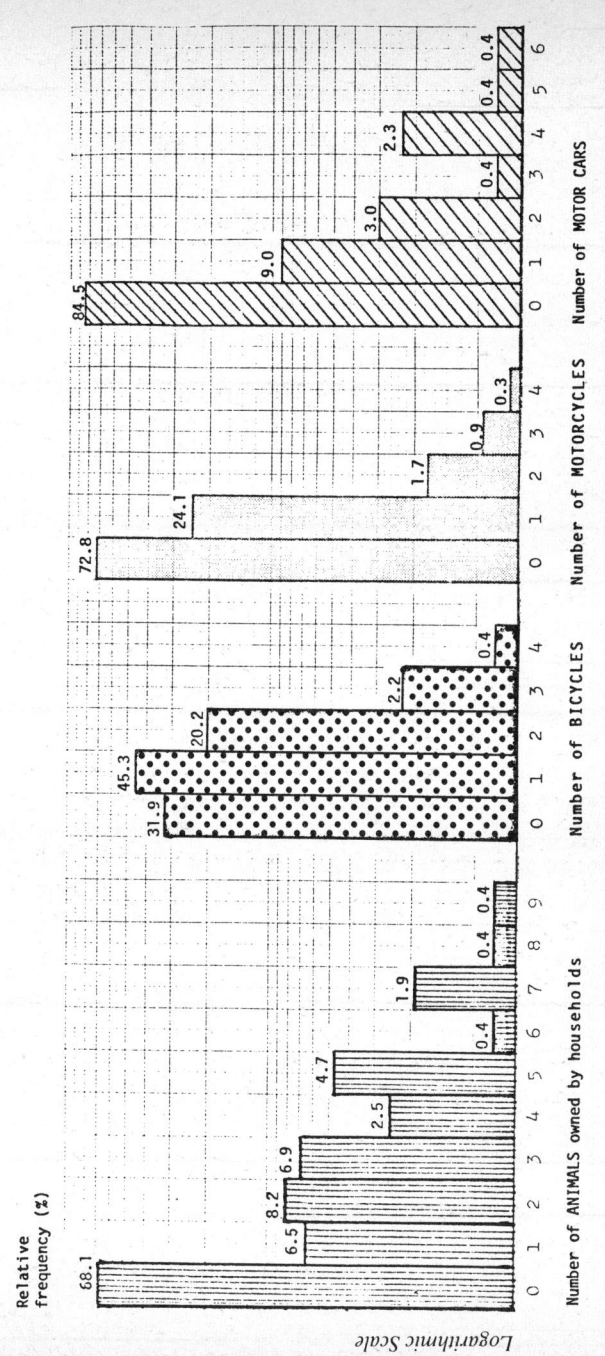

Fig. 4 *Frequency Distribution of Number of Animals, Bicycles, Motorcycles and Motor Cars owned by Households*

ation of the characteristics of households owning only bicycles shows that ownership of this vehicle is strongly influenced by income level. Households owning no vehicle at all have an average annual income of ₦1,335. Households owning one bicycle have an average annual income of ₦2,480, and those owning two bicycles ₦4,550. Households owning more than two bicycles also own at least one other type of vehicle. Another factor which affects vehicle ownership, certainly at the motorized level, relates to the social structure of Nigerian society. The wealth of a rich person is enjoyed, through the extended family system, by less fortunate relations who may not belong to the household. Although the data indicate that most farming households cannot afford to own motor vehicles, some of those owning one motor car have relatively low average incomes. This would be explained by well-to-do relations subsidizing the purchase and maintenance of the vehicle.

No evidence was obtained from the interviews of farmers obtaining loans from the commercial banks. This is hardly surprising since commercial banks have only recently begun to establish branches in rural areas. Furthermore the loan conditions imposed by these banks — good credit rating and property to serve as collateral — are likely to constitute insurmountable obstacles to poor rural households.

The main form of finance available to farming households is soft loans granted through special co-operative banks established by the Federal Government. These banks operate what is in essence a revolving loan scheme and grant loans to registered Co-operative Societies for distribution among their members. The amount of loan granted each year depends on available funds. Societies obtain the loan at the beginning of the planting season and are expected to pay back at the end of the harvesting season. Several Co-operative Societies arrange to sell members' crops collectively and repay the loans before returning the balance from the sales to their members.

The loan scheme is deficient in two ways as a means of financing the purchase of vehicles. The amount given to a farmer is often very small, and inadequate to purchase any vehicle. Second, even if adequate funds are available, the period of repayment is too short for poor farmers to contemplate borrowing an amount sufficient to buy a bicycle, which for them would be a major purchase.

The bicycle industry in Nigeria

Given the importance of the bicycle in rural transport in Nigeria, it is useful to examine the characteristics of the local manufacturing industry.

There are two bicycle manufacturers in Nigeria with a combined capacity of 500,000 units. As Table 22 shows, sales of bicycles declined steadily each year from 1977 to 1980, but rose substantially, though not to former levels, in 1981. More important, the share of the market taken by locally manufactured bicycles declined throughout the period so that by 1981 the industry was operating at only about 40 per cent of capacity. The major reason for this decline was the stiff competition from Indian imports. The import tariff on bicycles is 10 per cent of the total landed cost. At this rate Indian imports are cheaper than the locally manufactured products, though it is alleged that they have been subsidized by up to 50 per cent by the Indian Government. This illustrates the conflict between protecting and encouraging local industry on the one hand and the benefit to the consumer of making bicycles available at the lowest price.

The two bicycle manufacturers are located in major cities and employ about 1,000 people. Some rural households (estimated at less than 5 per cent) provide bicycle repair and maintenance services to supplement their income from farming. The average annual income from these services is ₦250-300.

Transportation and agriculture

Donkeys are used primarily for goods haulage and, as noted earlier, can be hired on a commercial basis. Their speed of travel is slow but they are hardy, resistant animals. However, keeping an animal purely for transportation needs does not, at the moment, make much economic sense. During the dry (off) season when the animal is little used for transport the owners are faced with the difficult task of fetching fodder for their animal The use of animals

Table 22. Details on Sales and Sources of Bicycles Sold in Nigeria

Year	Total Sales	Local manu-facture	Imports India	China	Japan	Others
1977	587,000	420,127	74,122	52,335	21,988	18,378
1978	488,000	343,188	77,621	25,697	14,000	27,494
1979	413,000	253,381	94,619	30,000	10,000	25,000
1980	315,000	185,000	57,000	35,000	19,000	19,000
1981	444,000	208,000	156,000	40,000	20,000	20,000

would be more economically attractive if they could also be used for agricultural purposes such as weeding and harvesting.

The bicycle has certain limitations in meeting the transport needs of farming households. Because the rider has to balance the vehicle it is not suitable for use by the elderly or very young, and it cannot be used to carry very heavy loads. However, the bicycle is relatively cheap, and hence widely available.

For trips to acquire farm inputs, all the farmers interviewed except those who own a motor vehicle use some form of public transport. They walk from their residence to the nearest point where they can board a public transport vehicle. Thus such trips involve out-of-pocket expenses for the farmer.

An overall assessment was made of the probable effect of transportation factors on the farmers' productivity. The interviewees were asked to rank, in order of importance, four key factors which had earlier been found [2] to have the most effect on farm productivity:

— *Ability to weed*: since most farmers in the country use hoes and knives to remove weeds the size of a household's total farm holdings is quite often based on its estimated weeding capabilities;
— *Transportation*: of seed to the farm and of the harvest to market;
— *Availability of sufficient land*: because of the complex land tenure system in the country, a household's total farm holdings may be limited by the type and size of land which is available to it;
— *Subsistence farming*: several households merely cultivate enough land to supply their food requirements, particularly if they have other sources of income. The farming output of such households would thus be based on their home consumption needs.

By applying scores to the rankings (i.e. one when ranked first, two when ranked second, etc.), multiplying these by the frequency of ranking, and aggregating the totals, total scores for each factor were obtained (Table 23).

With this method the factor with the lowest total score is the most important. However, the difference in total scores between factors does not indicate the degree of relative importance.

The table shows that transportation is less of a constraint than ability to weed and availability of land. The transport problems faced by farmers vary from one season to another. During the planting season, the main problem faced by farmers who do not

Table 23. Households' Ranking of the Production Factors

Factors			RANK			Total score	Rank
		1	2	3	4		
Ability to weed	Frequency	73	82	11	7		
	Aggregate score	73	164	33	28	298	1
Transportation	Frequency	8	32	121	12		
	Aggregate score	8	64	363	48	483	3
Availability of sufficient land	Frequency	84	46	30	13		
	Aggregate score	84	92	90	52	318	2
Subsistence Farming	Frequency	6	14	12	141		
	Aggregate score	6	28	36	564	634	4

own motor vehicles is the access time to, and cost of, public transport for trips to obtain inputs. During the farming and harvesting seasons, the trips made are primarily to and from the farm, and indeed these constitute the large majority of all movements by farming households. There are some indications that transport of farm products is not a particular problem for farmers. This appears to be because crops are commonly stored on the farm and transported in smaller quantities as and when required.

Given the view, well supported by interviewees, that existing available vehicles are not suitable to their needs, the surveyed farmers were asked to rank four vehicle attributes in order of importance:

— *Speed*: explained as the ability of the vehicle to convey the user to the destination within a reasonable time.

Table 24. Farmers' Rankings of their Preferences on Vehicles' Attributes

Factors		RANK 1	2	3	4	Total score	Overall Rank
Speed	Frequency	196	54	56	19		
	Aggregate score	196	108	168	76	548	1
Load carrying capacity	Frequency	56	228	29	12		
	Aggregate score	56	456	87	48	647	2
Reliability	Frequency	21	8	226	70		
	Aggregate score	21	16	678	280	995	3
Cost	Frequency	51	37	13	224		
	Aggregate score	51	74	39	896	1,060	4

— *Load carrying capacity*: explained as the capability of the vehicle to carry the user and all his loads;
— *Reliability*: explained as the ready availability of the vehicle at whatever time required;
— *Cost*: explained as the vehicle's capability to render required services with reasonably low total (i.e. both initial and operating) costs.

The results, using the rank scoring method described earlier, are presented in Table 24.

It is apparent that the farmers consider a vehicle's speed and load carrying capacity as its most useful attributes while reliability and cheapness are less important. This implies that the farmers would be willing to pay adequately for good service rather than owning their own vehicle. However, it is important to note that the data was obtained during the first questionnaire and therefore reflects the farmers' perceptions of effective solutions to their transportation problems during the planting season.

Summary

Economic realities preclude, for the foreseeable future, both the linking of every village and town by motorable road, and the widespread ownership of motor vehicles. However, there is potential for improving transport for farming households. For example, a government service to deliver farm inputs to the village for sale to the farmers would lessen the problems faced during the planting season. This would be an extension of the Government's present role in subsidizing fertilizers and improved seedlings.

The main problem for rural households would appear to be a general lack of individual access to the transport system. Many households do not own any form of transport. The bicycle, although it has certain limitations, is cheap, and simple to operate and maintain, and contributes to meeting the farmers' transport requirements. The provision of loans on terms that would enable poorer households to purchase bicycles would increase the availability of this form of transport. Finally, animals, particularly donkeys, could play a greater role in rural transport but are only likely to be more widely used when a greater proportion of households own them. This is only likely to occur if their use can be extended to weeding and harvesting.

CHAPTER 4

Transport in Two Kenyan Villages[†]

Introduction

The Kirinyaga District of Kenya is a densely populated, highly fertile agricultural area. Over the last 10 years this District, like many of the other heavily populated Districts of Kenya, has benefitted from the Government's attempts to provide improved access, in particular through the Rural Access Roads Programme.

The study on which this chapter is based was an attempt to compare the effect of contrasting levels of access on two villages in proximity to each other. The study focused on the level of vehicle ownership and on the methods and costs of moving farm produce to market and meeting other transport needs. It was carried out by Dr. Charles Kaira whilst he was at the Institute of Development Studies, the University of Nairobi.

The field work for the study was carried out in 1980. It took the form of a sample questionnaire and interview in the two villages. Certain biases were inherent in the sampling and an attempt has been made to take this into account in presenting the results of the study. The study is important in that it is one of the few that has attempted to identify travel demand at the local level.

Background

This case study is based on the findings of a household interview survey carried out in 1980 in two villages in the Mwea Division of Kirinyaga District in the Central Province of Kenya (Figure 5). Village A has relatively good access to road transport, while the centre of Village B is more than 6 km from the nearest road with a

---

[†]The study on which this chapter is based is described in Charles Kaira, *Transportation Needs of the Rural Population of Developing Countries: An Approach to Improved Transportation Planning*, Institut für Regionalwissenschaft der Universität Karlsruhe, April 1983. Exchange rate at the time of study K.Sh.7.4 (Kenya shillings) = US$1.0.

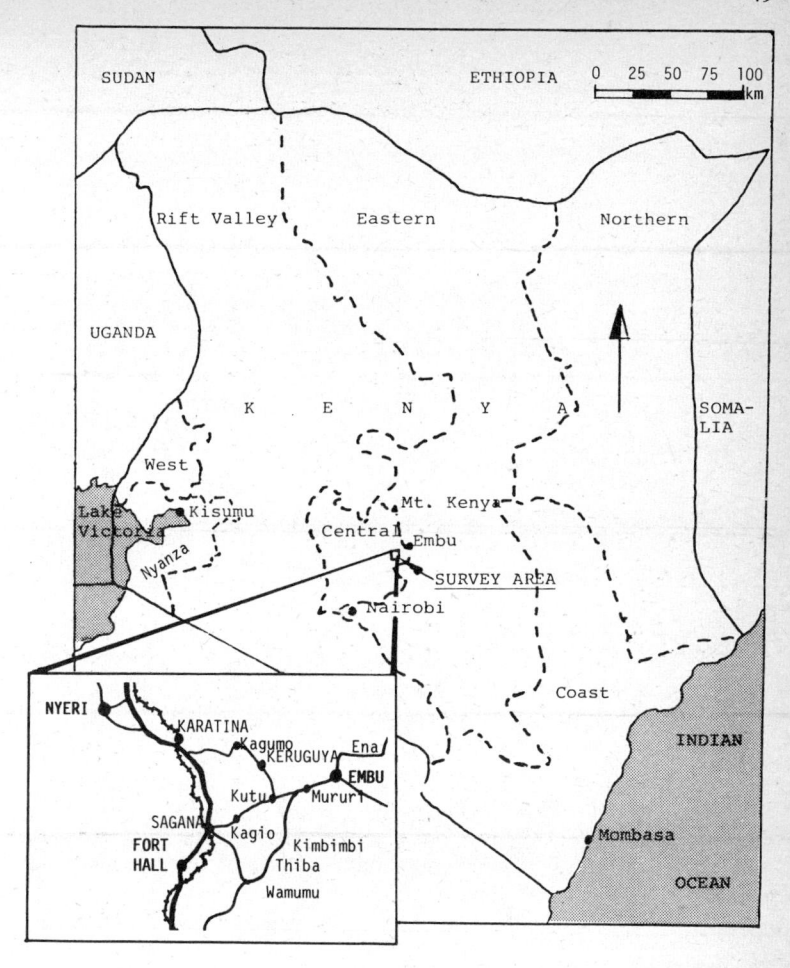

Fig. 5 *Map of Kenya*

dependable public transport service (Figure 6). Sixty-eight per cent of households in Village A, and 99 per cent in Village B are more than 2 km from the nearest market. However, both villages have relatively good access, in comparison with national planning targets, to dispensaries, water sources and primary schools.[1] The 30 per cent illiteracy rate in the area is similar to the national average, while the proportion of permanent dwellings in the two villages is well above the national target of 30 per cent. Formal employment in the area is negligible, and the large majority of households are engaged in smallholder agriculture.

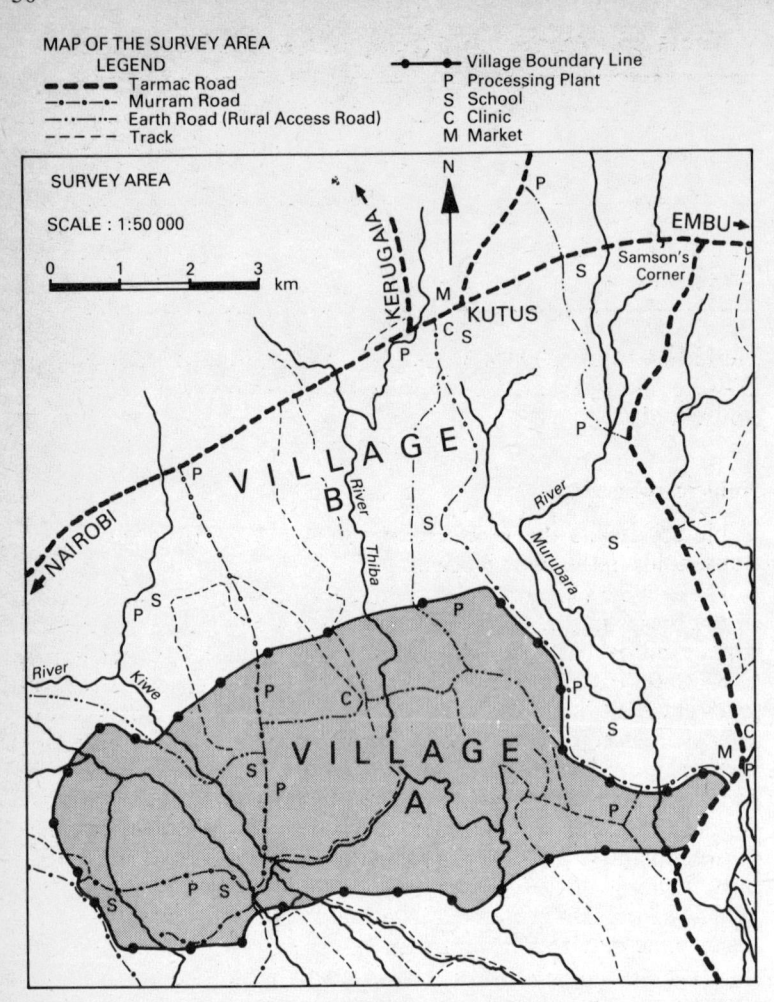

Fig. 6 *Map of the Survey Area*

In Village A, which is densely populated, survey interviews were carried out in every eighth household. In Village B, interviews were conducted with every fourth household. However when, among a set of four sample households, none owned a bicycle or donkey/ox cart, then one household amongst the sixteen which owned such a transport mode was interviewed. This introduces a bias into the sampling procedure but was necessary in order to collect sufficient data about these modes of transport. For similar reasons all households owning motor vehicles were inter-

Table 25. Vehicle Ownership in Sample Households

	Lorry	Car	Pick-up	Motor cycle	Donkey cart	ox cart	Bicycle	Wheel-barrow	Total vehicles	Number of households sampled
Village A	3	14	12	6	25	19	61	21	161	170
Village B	2	5	9	7	46	18	93	25	205	175

viewed. A total of 174 households in Village A and 176 in Village B were interviewed. There were, on average, 8.6 people per household.

Vehicle ownership

Table 25 details the numbers of vehicles owned by the sample households in the two villages.

These figures have to be interpreted with some caution. Because of the biases in the original sample they overestimate the proportion of animal carts and bicycles in Village B. They overestimate, to a greater extent, the proportion of motor vehicles in the two villages since all households owning these modes were interviewed. However, it can be concluded that the proportion of households owning motor vehicles is small, and that the most commonly owned vehicles are bicycles and animal carts. However, the sample biases prevent any conclusions being drawn on the relationship between vehicle ownership and access to the road network. Similarly, analysis of the relationship between household income and vehicle ownership is not possible because the study only generated data on income from sale of farm products. It is known that earnings from formal employment, and money repatriated by relatives working in towns, are significant contributions to total household income.

Of the bicycles owned by the sample households, about 35 per cent were purchased new, and 65 per cent second-hand. Over 96 per cent were bought for cash. In contrast, 97.5 per cent of the animal carts were purchased new, 87.5 per cent were bought for cash, but about 9.5 per cent were purchased on instalment terms. Table 26 details the cost of new bicycles and animal carts for the period 1976-79. Prices of second-hand bicycles are not available but would be cheaper than new ones and dependent on condition.

Bicycles are purchased new from traders in towns and second-

Table 26. Acquisition Costs for New Bicycles and Animal Carts in K.Sh.

Vehicle category	Years			
	1976	1977	1978	1979
Bicycle	650-850	650-850	850-1,200	1,000-1,300
Animal cart[1]	600-1,800	640-1,600	800-1,900	1,200-2,000

[1] Animal cart prices have a wide range because the price depends on the quality of the material (metal or wood) and workmanship.

hand from individuals, while animal carts are made to order by local craftsmen. The dominance of cash purchases reflects the fact that farmers do not normally have access to hire purchase facilities. Even if such facilities are available, farmers do not have the securities required. Analysis of responses to questioning on why households purchased their bicycles or animal carts at a particular time show that availability of cash was the major consideration:

— 80 per cent of the respondents answered 'That is when the household obtained enough money to pay for the vehicle';
— 10.5 per cent answered 'That is when the household realized the value of the vehicle as a general transporter in the household';
— 6 per cent answered 'The household needed another vehicle to replace the old one or to help the existing one';
— 3.5 per cent answered 'The vehicle was needed for business/ fieldwork transport'.

Since long life span and maximum utilization of a vehicle depend on its maintenance, the costs of maintaining a bicycle and an animal cart in rural conditions were investigated. In most cases it is the ability to pay which determines whether the vehicle is well maintained during its life span. The average annual cost of maintaining a bicycle in the study area is about K.Sh.220. No statistical difference in the cost of maintenance of bicycles of different ages was found. This analysis is complicated by the fact that it was difficult to determine the age of bicycles purchased second-hand. However, the data shows that, on average, replacement of tyres

Table 27. Cost of Maintaining Animal Carts

Age of cart in years	Average annual maintenance cost in K.Sh.
0- 5	190
6-10	280
Over 10	365

and inner tubes accounts for about 50 per cent of total maintenance costs. The design of animal carts is essentially the same whether they are drawn by oxen or donkeys, consisting of a body mounted on the discarded rear axle of a motor car. However the harness design depends on the type of draught animal. The average annual cost of maintaining an animal cart (excluding costs associated with the animal) is about K.Sh.280. There is some evidence that cost increases with the age of the cart, as Table 27 shows.

The major maintenance cost items are replacement or repair of tyres and wooden bodies. This is not surprising as in almost 100 per cent of the cases worn out or retreaded car tyres are used on the animal cart and untreated wood is used for building the body of the cart.

Transport of farm products to market

In the context of subsistence farming, four categories of farm products have been identified:

1 livestock and poultry,
2 dairy products,
3 foodcrops, and
4 perishable products (e.g. fruit and vegetables).

In the survey area, cattle, goats and sheep invariably move to the market under the guidance of an escort walking on foot. Pigs and rabbits are moved by animal cart. Milk, which is the only dairy product in the area, is transported on foot and by bicycle in 70 and 30 per cent of cases respectively. The quantities sold are usually very small (0.5 to 5 litres) and the distances travelled are normally less than 3 km though they may be up to 8 km. Since the sale of milk is a daily task, it is usually the child going to school or a household member going to work who carries the milk. Thus the trip is essentially dual purpose.

The three major cash crops grown in the main season are maize, beans and cotton, while the most important perishable crop is tomatoes.

Table 28 shows the distribution of sample households by weight of crops sold. As can be seen from the table, 88 and 83 per cent of the households respectively in Village A and Village B sold less than 500 kg of a single cash crop.

Table 29 details the charges for the two main means of hire transport available in the study area, animal carts and *matatu*. (A *matatu* is a share taxi, usually a station wagon or pick-up, with the rear body adapted to carry passengers and goods.)

As far as maize and beans are concerned, the animal cart charges in Village A are generally lower than those of the *matatus* while in Village B the charges for the two modes are similar. The possible explanation is that in Village B *matatus* operate only on market days for the purpose of transporting farmers and their farm

Table 28. Distribution of Households According to Sales by Weight of Cash Crops Grown in the Main Season

Type of crop	1-100	101-200	201-500	Over 500	Number of households
Village A					
Maize	6	9	9	8	32
Beans	17	8	3	1	29
Cotton	32	10	9	1	52
Tomato	2	1	—	3	6
Total	57	28	21	13	119
Village B					
Maize	19	9	17	15	60
Beans	22	5	4	7	38
Cotton	22	18	24	3	67
Tomato	4	3	3	4	14
Total	67	35	48	29	179

(Quantity sold in kilograms)

Table 29. Transport Charges in the Study Area (K.Sh.)

	Animal cart		Matatu	
	Maize/Beans	Cotton	Maize/Beans	Cotton
Village A	13[1] (9-17)[2]	51 (32-58)	26 (20-35)	—
Village B	11 (9-13)	45 (31-60)	13 (9-15)	16 (11-21)

[1] Average
[2] Range

products. However, in Village A *matatu* operation is mainly for passenger transport and operators try to keep away farmers travelling with farm products by imposing a high surcharge on the accompanied goods.

The table shows that the charges for cotton are much higher than for other crops. Cotton is a light but bulky product and therefore the transport cost, expressed in tonne/kilometres, is high compared with maize and beans which are dense.

The transport methods used for the three cash crops are very similar for the two villages. Over 70 per cent of the crops are moved by animal carts, which have low charges and are fairly widely owned in the villages, 17-19 per cent by *matatu* and the remainder by walking. These crops do not spoil easily and are normally sold either to co-operative stores, produce boards or private agencies where timeliness of delivery is not a factor.

In Village B, tomatoes are transported exclusively by *matatu*. In this village, *matatu* charges are comparable to those of the animal cart.

Furthermore, as tomatoes are sold only in the market, time is an important factor. However, in Village A which is nearer the markets and where the *matatu* charges are higher than those of the animal cart, only 20 per cent of the tomato crop is transported by *matatu*.

It is noteworthy that, except for milk delivery, crops are not transported to market by bicycle. This highlights the different roles of bicycles and animal carts, which are the most commonly owned vehicles and are of comparable cost. The bicycle is used for

Table 30. The Share by Weight in Kilograms of Transport of Farm Products to Market by Various Transport Modes

Type of crop	Walking	Animal cart	Matatu	Total
Village A				
Maize	630	8,820	2,100	11,550
Beans	425	2,190	1,045	3,660
Cotton	1,404	5,084	1,190	7,678
Total	2,459	16,094	4,335	22,888
Percentage	10.74	70.31	18.94	100.0
Tomatoes	—	4,080	1,080	5,160
Village B				
Maize	1,735	13,140	4,050	18,925
Beans	205	1,830	1,320	3,355
Cotton	1,502	9,835	400	11,737
Total	3,442	24,805	5,770	34,017
Percentage	10.11	72.91	16.96	100.0
Tomatoes	—	60	8,970	9,030

personal purposes such as travelling to and from work, visiting and shopping, while the animal cart is used as a load carrier.

Trip making by household members

The study included an analysis of the trip making characteristics of the sample households. Five categories of trip purpose were defined:

— work trips related to paid employment;
— shopping/markets;
— leisure activity — visiting, recreation, trips to hospital and church;
— farm activity — going to cultivate, grazing animals and transporting inputs/produce around the farm;

— household activities — washing clothes and bathing at the river bank, water and firewood collection.

Four categories of household members were defined and interviewed — father, mother, son and daughter.

Table 31 details the trips made per person per day. The data have to be interpreted with some caution since they are based on trips made by respondents on the day prior to being interviewed. They therefore do not reflect seasonal variations and in particular:

— exclude school trips as schools were closed at the time of the study;

Table 31. Trips per Person per Day According to Family Status and Trip Purpose

Trip purpose	Father	Mother	Son	Daughter	All
Village A					
Sample size	95	127	74	64	360
Work	0.24	0.02	0.07	0.02	0.09
Shopping/marketing	0.62	0.23	0.31	0.27	0.36
Leisure activity	0.51	0.36	0.49	0.28	0.41
Farm activity	0.27	0.49	0.57	0.58	0.46
Household activity	0.27	0.29	0.27	0.31	0.29
Total	1.91	1.39	1.71	1.46	1.61
Village B					
Sample size	132	147	89	83	451
Work	0.13	0.03	0.12	0.04	0.08
Shopping/marketing	0.59	0.44	0.28	0.23	0.41
Leisure activity	0.59	0.35	0.53	0.47	0.49
Farm activity	0.59	0.59	0.71	0.35	0.57
Household activity	0.08	0.63	0.21	0.49	0.36
Total	1.98	2.04	1.85	1.58	1.91

— marketing trips are much fewer than would be expected at harvest time;
— interviews in Village A were conducted during the rainy season when the number of trips to collect water decreases.

However the data do illustrate the range of trip purposes and the roles of different members of the household. The survey showed marked variation in the use of transport modes by different members of the household. Mothers or daughters rarely use bicycles, probably on the grounds of custom or life-style. Fathers, who usually control the household cash, make more trips by public transport than other members.

Table 32 shows the modal distributions of all trips in the two villages. What is of significance is the predominance of walking as a means of transport. For shopping and leisure trips, for instance, walking is the most common mode, accounting for 60-80 per cent of trips, the remainder being by bicycle or *matatu*. Over 80 per cent of trips for these purposes are less than 7 km, suggesting that they are usually within the village neighbourhood. The different levels of access to road transport in the two villages have no significant effect on this.

Table 33 shows the distribution of walking trips in relation to farm and household trips. Of particular interest here is the fact that loaded walking trips (head or backloading) account for one in three of all trips and that 95 per cent of those loaded trips are carried out by women and children. About 70 per cent of trips involving carrying a load are for water collection. The usual loads are about 25 kg and the distances range from 0 to 8 km. Both water and firewood collection are female activities. It is apparent that, apart from transport of farm products during harvest, water collection poses the major daily transport problem to the subsistence farmer.

Table 32. Percentage Distribution of Trips by Mode

	Walking	Animal cart	Bicycle	Public transport	Other	Total
Village A	72.0	1.5	7.5	7.5	11.5	100.0
Village B	71.0	6.0	10.5	7.5	5.0	100.0
Average	71.5	4.5	9.0	7.5	7.5	100.0

Table 33. A Breakdown of Farm and Household Walking Trips According to Family Status

	Family status					
Trip purpose	Father	Mother	Son	Daughter	All	%
Village A						
Sample size	95	127	74	64	360	8
FARM:						
Graze animals	5	1	12	2	20	8
Cultivate	18	58	28	33	137	55
Farm transport[1]	1	3	2	3	9	4
Sub-total	24	62	42	38	166	67
HOUSEHOLD:						
Wash clothes	—	—	—	2	2	1
Bathe	7	1	16	2	26	10
Collect water[1]	1	28	2	12	43	17
Collect firewood[1]	—	7	—	4	11	4
Sub-total	8	36	18	20	82	32
Total	32	98	60	58	248	99
Trips per day	0.34	0.77	0.81	0.91	0.69	
Village B						
Sample size	132	147	89	83	451	
FARM:						
Graze animals	22	15	21	5	63	15
Cultivate	42	57	40	18	157	38
Farm transport[1]	9	14	2	6	31	8
Sub-total	73	86	63	29	251	61
HOUSEHOLD:						
Wash clothes	1	4	1	2	8	2
Bathe	7	—	14	4	25	6
Collect water[1]	—	72	3	28	103	25
Collect firewood[1]	—	15	—	7	22	5
Sub-total	8	91	18	41	158	38
Total	81	177	81	70	409	99
Trips per day	0.61	1.20	0.91	0.84	0.91	

[1] Trips that involve carrying loads.

Summary

The study was intended to show the differences in transport demand related to two levels of access. This it did only to a limited extent. Vehicle ownership was similar as was the amount of cash crops sold. Transport costs did vary although the variation was difficult to ascribe merely to the level of access. On the other hand, the study does say a great deal about the actual demand for travel in the villages in general. Transport for agricultural activity is not dominant, trips for leisure and household activities are equally important. The majority of transport takes place on foot. Trip lengths are short and loads are light and predominantly carried on the back. Each member of the household makes one and a half to two trips per day. The trips for marketing or shopping represent only 20-25 per cent of the total but will generally not be on foot. They take place on animal carts, bicycles or public transport.

PART II — TRANSPORT MEANS

CHAPTER 5

Means of Transport in Western Samoa[†]

Introduction

Western Samoa suffers from many of the typical problems of Pacific developing countries. A combination of topography, scattered territory, an inability to exploit economies of scale in manufacturing and a relatively poor industrial base restrict the choice of means whereby goods can be moved without relying on imported technologies.

The study upon which this chapter is based was commissioned by the Government with the objective of investigating the most appropriate rural transport technology to meet village agricultural needs in Western Samoa. It was carried out by Ian Barwell in 1980 by means of a detailed survey supported by secondary data.

Background

The country consists of two major islands, Upolu and Savai'i, and five smaller islands, only two of which are inhabited. The capital, and only urban centre in the country, is Apia on Upolu Island. The total population is 160,000, of which 25 per cent live in or around Apia, 50 per cent in other parts of Upolu, and 25 per cent in Savai'i. Thus about 75 per cent of the population of Samoa lives in rural areas. There are about 360 villages on the two major islands with typical populations of 200-500. Most of the villages are situated around the coasts with the cultivated plantations located inland.

The rural economy is predominantly agricultural, crops being

[†]This chapter is based on work for the Government of Western Samoa by Ian Barwell. At the time of the study 1$ (Samoan Tala) = US$1.14.

produced to meet family requirements with the surplus sold for consumption within Samoa or for export. The Government's development policy recognizes that Samoa will remain a largely rural village-based society and therefore a major objective is to increase production in village agriculture. The major crops grown at present are copra, taro, cocoa and bananas, while fishing is also an important source of food for family consumption and for sale.

The economic situation in Samoa restricts expansion in the use of motor vehicles, and has therefore increased the need to give attention to technologies utilizing local resources. The country has a substantial balance of payments deficit, and foreign exchange controls imposed as a result of this have severely restricted the availability of imported motor vehicles. Petroleum products account for about 8 per cent of the total value of imports, and the operating costs of motor vehicles have risen substantially because of increases in the retail prices of petrol and diesel fuel.

The experience gained since the inception of the Rural Development Programme in 1977 suggested that the horses found in most village communities in the country might be utilized more efficiently to reduce the time and effort devoted to meeting the transportation requirements of village agriculture. In particular, it was considered that the introduction of more efficient means of transport between village and plantation would contribute to increasing productivity.

Transport in Western Samoa

The nature and problem of rural transport in Samoa are conditioned by certain specific characteristics of the country. These include its small size, the nature of the road system, the location of the villages close to the major road network but separate from the cultivated plantations, and the lack of a significant regional marketing structure.

Western Samoa has a fairly good major rural road system. Upolu has sealed roads running along most of the north and south coast, and three cross-island roads of which two are sealed. Savai'i has a coast road running right around the island which is sealed where it passes through villages. Minor 'radial' roads or tracks provide access to those villages not situated adjacent to the major roads and, more importantly, link villages to their cultivated plantations. The current Access Roads Programme is aimed at improving access to inland areas and some 1,300 km have already been constructed or upgraded under the scheme.

It is possible to define two distinct elements of rural transport:
— village-market
— village-plantation

Village-market transport
'Village-market' transport includes all those journeys which involve travel outside the village and plantation area, for example to sell cash crops, to purchase agricultural inputs and household articles, and for social and educational purposes. Such journeys are carried out predominantly using motorized transport.

There are 4,070 motor vehicles licensed for road use in Western Samoa, 3,570 on Upolu and 500 on Savai'i. Thus the average motor vehicle density is about 25 motor vehicles/1,000 population, though in Savai'i the figure is much lower at 12.5/1,000.

There is no publicly-owned passenger transport system, all bus services being provided by private operators. Many of the 150 buses currently licensed are operated by village-based individuals or groups and provide a service to and from the home village. Substantial quantities of accompanied goods are carried by passengers on buses, the average load brought into Apia market being about 80 kg.

The light pick-up of about 1 tonne nominal payload capacity is the most common motor vehicle in the country. There is at least one pick-up owned in most of the villages and it serves as a general purpose carrier of people and cargo. Motor cars and trucks are less commonly owned in villages than pick-ups, and there is only a very limited commercial trucking service available.

While there is a limited amount of inter-village trading, cash crops for domestic consumption are marketed predominantly in Apia, and, to a lesser extent at Salaelologa on Savai'i. The major means of transport for the marketing of cash crops for domestic consumption are the pick-up and bus. A 1976 survey of Apia market[1] showed that 49 per cent of produce was brought to market by pick-up, 33 per cent by bus and the remainder by car. The same modes are used for personal transport to purchase goods, or for social purposes. Export crops are normally sold by the producer at the village to a local trader, who is then responsible for the transport and re-sale of the produce in Apia. The major modes of transport are the pick-up and truck.

Because of the nature of crop marketing, the emphasis of village-market transport is on travel to and from Apia and Salaelologa, often over a considerable distance. This limits the potential application of low-cost forms of transport for village-market journeys.[2] If and when a regional marketing structure develops, the consequent reduction in typical travel distances would increase the potential for these forms of transport.

Village-plantation transport
Village-plantation transport includes all those journeys which involve travel around the area of the village and plantations, and in particular:

— movement of labour, materials (e.g. planting materials, fertilizer) and implements (e.g. digging sticks, knapsack sprayers), from the village to the plantation;
— movement of harvested crops, labour and implements from the plantation to the village; and
— collection of materials for household and social purposes (e.g. firewood, building materials).

The two traditional, and still the most common, methods of transport are walking and the pack-horse. The traditional means of carrying loads when walking is with a shoulder pole, which has the load attached at one or both ends, one person being able to carry up to 25-35 kg.

The most recent survey of the horse population, carried out in 1963, indicated 2,140 village-owned horses distributed equally between Upolu and Savai'i. Discussions suggest that there has not been any substantial change since 1963. While there are several horses owned in most of the villages on the two islands, they are banned by a few communities for social reasons. The horses are used to carry cargo loads, including crops and firewood, and people. Loads of up to a maximum of 135 kg are carried. The harness arrangement consists simply of a rope tied around the horse's neck and mouth. Cargo is carried in low slung burlap panniers, while the rider sits on a burlap cloth sometimes padded with grass. Village horses are small (most are in fact ponies) and are locally bred. While there is considerable variation in the condition of the horses, generally they are not particularly well fed.

People with access to pick-ups use them for village-plantation transport where there are suitable roads. The Government has recently introduced a tractor-trailer hire service. Eighteen tractor-trailer units, with nominal payload capacity of 2 tonnes, are distributed through the two major islands and are available for hire, with operator, at a subsidized rate of $3.20 per hour ($25.60 per day). No detailed analysis of the utilization of these units has yet been carried out, but estimates indicate that they are in use for about two full days per week.

The type of agriculture practised in Samoa, and particularly the emphasis on crops such as copra which yield a substantial weight of produce, results in significant village-plantation transport requirements. Furthermore, the transportation effort involved in clearing, cultivating and harvesting a plantation is increasing as land more distant from the village is brought into production. This has proved necessary because of the declining fertility of land close to the village and in order to increase crop production for domestic consumption by a growing population and for export.

An indication of the transport requirements of village agriculture can be obtained from analysis of the results of a survey of a 'typical copra and cocoa selling farm family' carried out by the Department of Agriculture in 1977.

The family surveyed worked six separate plots of land:

— two old coconut plantations totalling 4.5 ha, intercropped with two acres of cocoa, located close to the village;
— two young coconut plantations, totalling 3.2 ha, 1.6 km distant from the village;
— 0.2 ha taro and taamu plantation, 2.4 km from the village;
— 0.1 ha taro plantation, 4.8 km from the village.

Based on the data given in the survey, the estimated transport requirements for movement of crops back to the village were as given below in Table 34.

Table 34. Transport Requirements of Village Agriculture

	Weight of harvested crop (tonne/annum)	Transport requirement for movement of crop to village (tonne-km/annum)
Case 1: existing conditions	46	36
Case 2: all coconuts harvested and moved to village prior to de-husking	65	50
Case 3: increased output of coconuts	94	96

The three cases require some explanation. Case 1 represents the existing volume of transport involved in moving the produce of a typical family farm back to the village. Case 2 is modified by two assumptions:

— that all coconuts are collected from the plantation. At present this is not usually done, a major reason being the effort involved;
— that all husks are brought back to the village. At present a substantial proportion of coconuts are de-husked in the plantation to reduce the weight to be transported. However, the Government is encouraging the export of coir fibre which will give the husk a commercial value.

Case 3 also allows for the increase in crop harvest which will occur when the young plantations on the farm reach maturity. Thus Case 3 represents the volume of crop transport involved if a typical family is to maximize its harvest.

This analysis demonstrates clearly the substantial transportation element involved in moving harvested produce from a typical family farm back to the village. It also demonstrates the additional transport requirement that results from efforts to increase agricultural production through more intensive cultivation of plantations and the use of land more distant from the village. The analysis covers only the movement of harvested produce to the village. This is the major transport requirement in terms of weight of cargo to be moved. However, to this must be added the considerable time and effort involved in travelling to the plantation to clear, cultivate and harvest the land, and the on-plantation transport involved in collecting coconuts.

The modes currently used to meet these transport needs lie at two extremes of the range of possible options. The two traditional modes, walking and pack-horse, are slow and have limited payloads, so that labour productivity is low, though the modes are widely available since the monetary costs involved are also low. Pick-ups and tractor-trailers have much higher payloads and can travel at higher speeds, so that labour productivity is higher. However, pick-ups are very expensive to purchase, and increasingly costly to operate because of rising fuel costs. Consequently they are beyond the means of most rural farming families (availability of pick-ups in rural areas is of the order of 1 vehicle/80-150 people). The hire scheme for tractor-trailers removes the barrier of high investment cost from the farmer but, even at a subsidized rate of $3.20/hr, the cost of using this mode is high. Thus it is logical to examine the potential for intermediate modes of transport, more productive than the traditional methods, but less costly and therefore more accessible to village families, than motorized vehicles.

Potential for horse-drawn carts
There is considerable potential for animal-powered means of transport. Horses are already widely available, and produce about ten times the power output of human beings. Further, the use of horses as the source of power for transport reduces the human physical effort involved in this activity. The way in which horses are used at present to carry loads on their backs is simple, and requires minimal monetary investment. Village horses change hands for $10-50 though often they are traded for goods or livestock rather than cash. The equipment required for a pack-horse (rope harness, panniers etc.) can be obtained very cheaply. However, except on very steep terrain the power output of a horse is more efficiently utilized by transferring the cargo load from its back to a wheeled cart. Horse-drawn carts can be expected to operate, with a reasonable load, on rising gradients of up to 10 per cent, but not on long continuous climbs. The terrain in most parts of Western Samoa is suitable for horse-drawn carts, particularly since in practice the heaviest loads, harvested crops, will be moved downhill from the plantation to the village rather than uphill. Moreover, the plantation roads being constructed under the Access Roads Programme are generally suitable for use by horse-drawn carts. The areas of the country where the terrain is likely to prove too steep for horse-drawn carts are parts of eastern Upolu and north-west Savai'i.

As noted earlier the village horses are small and are generally not particularly well fed, though they are hardy and disease resistant. The introduction of carts would, initially at least, be aimed at using the horses' energy more efficiently, rather than at substantially increasing the work load demanded of them. In the longer term, efforts to improve the quality of the animals, by the introduction of new breeding stock and better feeding methods, would increase the workload of which they were capable. Under present conditions horse-drawn carts can be expected to carry loads of up to a maximum of about 400 kg plus driver.

Table 35 compares the characteristics of the horse-drawn cart with the traditional modes of walking and pack-saddle horses, light pick-ups and tractor-trailers. It is based on the following assumptions:

- walking — load 32 kg, average speed 4.8 km/h
- horse carrying rider and cargo load — load 57 kg, average speed 6.4 km/h
- horse carrying cargo load with handler walking alongside — load 125 kg, average speed 6.4 km/h
- horse-drawn cart carrying driver — load 400 kg, average speed 4 km/h
- light pick-up — load 1 tonne, average speed on access road 24 km/h
- tractor-trailer — load 2 tonnes, average speed on access road 11 km/h

The cost of acquiring a cart, which gives an indication of its availability to rural families, is much lower than that of a pick-up. It is expected that the purchase of carts would be funded through the Rural Development Programme which would reduce the cost by 50 per cent to about $250. The introduction of the tractor-trailers hire scheme means that there is no 'investment' cost associated with this mode of transport. However the hire charge, at $25.60 per day, is high. The annual cost of owning a cart, allowing for depreciation, interest charges and maintenance, is estimated at about $65, equivalent to two and a half days hire of a tractor-trailer.

Horse-drawn carts offer a substantial increase in transport capacity and reduction in physical effort involved compared with the traditional modes. The saving in effort is important since the

Table 35. Characteristics of Village-plantation Transport Modes

Mode	Investment cost $	Cargo carrying capacity tonne km/hour
Walking	0	0.15
Horse (cargo and rider)	10-50	0.36
Horse (cargo only)	10-50	0.80
Horse-drawn cart	420-570[1]	2.56
Light pick-up	8-9,000[2]	24.00
Tractor-trailer	0	22.00

[1] Cost of cart, harness and horse.
[2] New vehicle.

effort involved in crop collection and transport is one of the factors that limits harvested output. Based on Case 3 described earlier, it would take 19 man-days to bring the crop to the village by horse-drawn cart, compared with 320 by walking and 102 by pack-horse (the last figure assumes the farmer rides his horse for 50 per cent of the time). Thus compared with the pack-horse there is a time saving of over 80 man-days per annum from the use of a horse-drawn cart for a cost of about $65. The benefit to the farmer depends on how the time is used. As one example, it is estimated that on a typical family farm 10-20 per cent of the coconut crop, with a value of $75-150, is left in the plantation and not harvested.

In addition to carrying crops back to the village, horse-drawn carts would be suitable for the transport of labour, equipment and materials to and from the plantation and for the collection of firewood and building materials. They could also be used for short journeys outside the village on major roads. However in most circumstances they would not be suitable for movement around copra plantations because of the placing of the trees and ground conditions. An alternative horse-drawn method of transport is the sledge, which could be hauled around a plantation more easily than a cart, and would be very cheap to manufacture. However on the surfaces typically found on access roads it is unlikely that a horse could move a significantly larger load on a sledge than on its back.

At present, circumstances in Samoa are very favourable for the introduction of horse-drawn carts. A number of organizations have expressed interest in and support for the concept including the Ministry of Transport and the Department of Agriculture. Several of the large commercial estates have also shown interest in using horse-drawn carts. At present tractor-trailers are used to move produce from the estates, but the operating costs are becoming prohibitive as fuel prices rise. The commercial estates already make considerable use of horses in their operations and have imported breeding stock to improve the quality of their animals which are larger, stronger and better cared for than the village horses.

Summary

The study indicated the potential for the use of an intermediate technology which would both contribute to removing transport constraints and to reducing the need to import the alternative — tractors and trailers. While the investigation indicated that there was considerable interest in their use, the acceptability and demand for horse-drawn carts among rural families can only be proven by a programme to introduce this form of transport. Thus the study does not prove that horse carts are the most appropriate choice, but it does demonstrate that there is a choice available for exploration.

CHAPTER 6

Improving Traditional Means of Transport in the Republic of Korea[†]

Introduction

The Republic of Korea is not generally considered as a low-income developing country — it has a GNP per capita similar to Malaysia for instance. Nevertheless, the rural area still provides the livelihood of a large proportion of its population. Given the difficulty of the terrain and the fact that only 20 per cent of the Republic's land is cultivable, the transport system has some unique features. Predominant among these, in the rural areas, is the *chee-geh*, a traditional load carrying frame.

This chapter describes work carried out at Soong Jun University to improve the efficiency of the *chee-geh*. Not only was this of interest in that little work of this nature has been done elsewhere but also because of the methodology adopted. A group comprising academics, artisans and farmers followed the study from conceptual design to the development of a commercially feasible product.

The work was carried out in collaboration with the Georgia Institute of Technology under the overall direction of Dr. Seyeul Kim with a grant from USAID.

Background

The *chee-geh* is a traditional load-carrying frame which is worn on the back and is unique to the Republic of Korea.[1] In spite of the fact that China and Japan have similar terrain and agricultural methods, nothing resembling the *chee-geh* has emerged there.

[†]The study on which this chapter is based is described in Seyeul Kim: *A Case Study on the Possibility of Improving the Simple Traditional Farm Equipment in Korea with Special Reference to the Chee-geh*. (Taejon, Republic of Korea, Regional Development Institute, Soong Jun University, February 1977.) Exchange rate at the time of the study 480W (Won) = US$1.0.

The evolution of the *chee-geh* in the Republic of Korea is believed to be related to that country's harsh winter climate, predominantly mountainous terrain, fragmented farming land, and narrow and undulating movement routes, all of which favour its use. For many years the people have burned firewood in their 'ondol' (flues that carry the hot gases of a fire — usually the kitchen fire — under the floor of the main rooms) heating systems. Therefore they frequently needed to haul wood to their villages from the mountains, often for long distances. Since 80 per cent of the land is unfarmable mountain terrain, the remaining arable portion is small and comprises numerous irregular pieces of land. There are also many small and large streams. The combination of these factors means that most of the roads and paths between village and field are narrow and winding. There is often little choice but human load carriage on the head or back.

Structure of the *chee-geh*

The traditional *chee-geh* is made mostly of wood, which is readily available from the pine trees growing in rural areas. Because the natural crotches of the trees are used for making the *chee-geh*, its construction is relatively simple (see Plate 5).

Every part of the *chee-geh* looks simple, but it can only carry heavy loads efficiently when it is well-balanced. The basic attachments are a basket and staff. The basket is used to carry loads made up of small pieces (such as fruit and vegetables). For very finely divided loads such as ashes or manure, a piece of matting is used to line the basket and prevent leakage. The staff is used to prop the *chee-geh* when it is standing alone.[2]

The traditional *chee-geh* takes somewhat different forms in different parts of the country, there being variations in the number of crossbars, attachment of the backpad, relative lengths above and below the fork, overall length and curvature of the frame, width of rear extensions and legs, and position of the shoulder strap. These differences between areas are probably due largely to variations in the type of terrain. Where the land is flat it is possible to carry a bulkier load so the upper part of the frame is longer than the lower part. On steep mountain trails loads must be less bulky so farmers prefer a generally smaller version. Frames in use on the plains have long legs to make it easier for the carrier to get it up on to his back when there is no slope in the ground to assist him. In some hilly areas the *chee-geh* is adapted for geater mobility: the lower end of the shoulder strap is attached high up, just below the backpad, and the upper end is attached just above the backpad.

Table 36. Average Yearly Income

Income (1,000W)	Number of people	%
Below 240	8	6.6
240-360	25	20.7
360-480	22	18.2
480-600	21	17.3
600-720	29	24.0
Above 720	15	12.4
No answer	1	0.8

Thus, although the *chee-geh* seems simple, it has been very carefully modified to suit the physical character of the land and the body structure of the user so that it will be of maximum utility.

Traditional *chee-geh* use

Interviews were carried out with 121 typical farm homes distributed among plains, intermediate and mountainous areas. Analysis showed there to be no significant differences in the responses from the three areas so their results were combined.

Table 36 shows the distribution of income characteristics and Table 37 the distribution of farm sizes among the sample population.

All of the farmers questioned used a *chee-geh* and 95 per cent said that it was necessary for their work. The study also showed

Table 37. Area of Land Cultivated

Area in hectares	Number of people	%
Very small scale (tenant farming)	7	5.8
Less than 0.3	12	9.9
0.3-0.7	33	27.3
0.7-1.0	34	28.2
1.0-1.3	17	14.0
More than 1.3	17	14.0
No answer	1	0.8

Table 38. Reasons Given for the Necessity of the *Chee-geh* in Farming

Reason	Number of people	%
Farm paths too narrow for hand cart or ox cart	51	44.3
No way to haul on mountain trails except *chee-geh*	49	42.7
Loads can be carried in fields and (rice) paddies	10	8.7
No hand cart available	5	4.3

(Table 38) that with the lack of adequate farm roads and difficult terrain there was no practical substitute for the *chee-geh*. In terms of most frequently carried loads, barley or rice, firewood, manure and grass were the main items, in descending order of frequency.

An analysis of the ability of farmers to carry various loads showed that 26 per cent could carry between 51-61 kg, and 23 per cent could carry from 71-80 kg. Although there were extreme variations 87 per cent were able to carry maximum loads ranging from 31-80 kg. Surprisingly, load-carrying ability did not seem to vary a great deal between the age of 30 and 60, experience and practice being the deciding factor.

In terms of the frequency of daily use, 26 per cent used it less than 5 times, 27 per cent between 5 and 10 times and 47 per cent more than 11 times a day. These figures emphasize the importance of the *chee-geh's* role in farming.

In terms of distance carried, the largest group, 20 per cent, carried their *chee-geh* between 8 to 10 km per day. This suggested that farmers spend a substantial proportion of their time and strength carrying loads on their backs, as a 10 km journey was estimated to occupy about 2 hours.

Another common form of farm transport is the *li-uh-ka* (metal handcart with spoked wheels). Surveys showed that while the handcart can haul a larger load than the *chee-geh*, and as a wheeled device is easy to use, it is uneconomic for small loads and required two or more people for large loads. Use by women or the old was also difficult. Thirty-one per cent of the farmers interviewed owned a *li-uh-ka*. A significant proportion of farmers (36 per cent) indicated that they could not afford a handcart and others (15 per cent) that it was unsuited to bad farm roads (Plate 6).

Although farmers were nearly unanimous that use of the *chee-geh* was inevitable because of its 'convenience on narrow, mountain and steep trails and in the fields and paddies' — 98 per cent felt it was still important as a transport device — most (91 per cent) also felt that as a primitive and troublesome device it should be discarded. This ambivalent attitude amoung farmers was the main reason for the conclusion that 'although the *chee-geh* is primitive and inconvenient, because it is absolutely necessary for farming, modern technology must be applied to modernize it'.

Development of an Improved *Chee-geh*

The method of developing an improved *chee-geh* consisted of a series of some eight 'development conferences' spread out over a 16-month period in 1975-1976. Participants in the conferences comprised *chee-geh* users (farmers), manufacturers and academics drawn from technical disciplines. The aim was to develop gradually an improved *chee-geh* based on the synthesis of potential ideas derived from the respective knowledge and experience of the conference participants. Six farmers (two each from lowland, intermediate and mountainous regions), three metal workers with long experience in *chee-geh* and farm-equipment manufacture, two medium-industry machine manufacturers, four professors of mechanical engineering, economics and management, two technical high school teachers (altogether 17 members) constituted the conferences which involved seven model-development meetings, two field surveys and their respective review and analysis meetings.

In order to investigate a wide range of opinions from the farmers especially, a different group of farmers was invited to each conference. Also, in the field tests of the progressively improved models, local community leaders and many influential people of all ages were asked to participate. Their opinions were recorded and immediately after each field test the results were closely analysed and summarized for review at the next meeting.

The conferences aimed at unearthing the participants' 'hidden ideas' through a process of free-association. Ideas presented, opinions and matters of discussion were recorded and then compiled by the conference chairman (research director) for report and re-examination at the next conference. On this basis the participating manufacturers eventually made test models which were field tested. The results of each field test were reported in the following conference, beginning with a close analysis of items pointed out by the farmers. A next-stage model would then be designed and in this step-by-step fashion, the conference progressed.

In all, six models were produced and tested before a satisfactory improved *chee-geh* resulted. The main feature of the new model was the addition of a pair of wheels (Plate 7) so that it might be pushed or pulled when the condition of the route surface permitted. Thus, the improved *chee-geh* combines some of the utility of the traditional device and the *li-uh-ka* (handcart). Addition of the wheels and construction in steel necessarily made the new model somewhat heavier than traditional *chee-geh*. Prior to finalizing the design, the improved *chee-geh* was subjected to evaluation by 100 farmers, to whom models were loaned for a brief period. They reacted positively to the improved *chee-geh* and gave user criticisms which were utilized in finalizing the design. The trials indicated that the increase in weight did not make the design less convenient since, whenever possible, it was wheeled rather than carried. A separate comparative trial between the new and traditional models — involving the transport of a 60 kg bag of grain over distances up to 3.5 km — indicated that the new model gave rise to significant time savings and productivity increases.

As part of the evaluation, farmers were asked at what price they would buy the improved *chee-geh*. Sixty-eight per cent said they would buy it at about half the price of a *li-uh-ka*, which is about three times the price of a traditional *chee-geh*.

Summary

The work at Soong Jun University shows what can be done when science is applied to the improvement of a traditional technology. The new version was acceptable to the users. Since the development work was completed, a number of potential manufacturers have expressed interest in the making of the new model. Nevertheless, they did not feel sufficiently confident to go into full-scale production without external assistance. As with many 'appropriate technologies' the missing link was the effective marketing of the product.

The concept of the *chee-geh* is one that is applicable to many other countries, and not just those with similar terrain types. The principle is sound and, where wood is not available, other materials such as steel tubing could be used. However, although superficially it seems simple, closer examination reveals that its efficiency results from a number of subtle design features.

CHAPTER 7

Means of Transport in the Philippines[†]

Introduction

The Philippines is well known for the ingenuity of its people. This is nowhere better reflected than in the diversity of transport vehicles available. These cater for the needs of different levels of society. In addition to conventional motor vehicles, they range from carabao(buffalo)-drawn sleds to the modified jeep known as the 'jeepney'. This case study, commissioned by the ILO, compares the most common forms of transport in one particular area of the Philippines. The objective of the study was to present a description of the transport situation as it pertains to the mass of the population of this particular area. No attempt was made to evaluate the best means of transport, nor to propose changes in policy or procedures which would assist rural transport.

The study focuses on jeepneys, trimobiles (motor-cycles fitted with sidecars), railway skates and *carabao* sleds. The study, carried out by Prof. R.B. Ocampo of the University of the Philippines is based on field interview data obtained in the first half of 1982. A total of 63 informants were interviewed. Thirty-nine of these were vehicle users, drivers, and owners for whom a common interview guide was prepared. The rest were vehicle-body builders and other key informants who were interviewed less formally, but in many cases just as extensively. The interview data were complemented by field observations, and by information from reports on road improvement and agricultural development projects in the study area, an interim report on transport in the region, and a previous evaluation study directed by Professor Ocampo.

Background

Some 70 per cent of the Philippines' 47 million population live in the rural areas. They depend for their livelihood on agriculture

[†]The study on which this chapter is based is described in R.B. Ocampo: *Rural Transport in the Philippines*, (Geneva, November 1982; mimeographed ILO World Employment Programme research Working Paper; restricted). Exchange rate at time of study P8.2 (Pesos) = US$1.0.

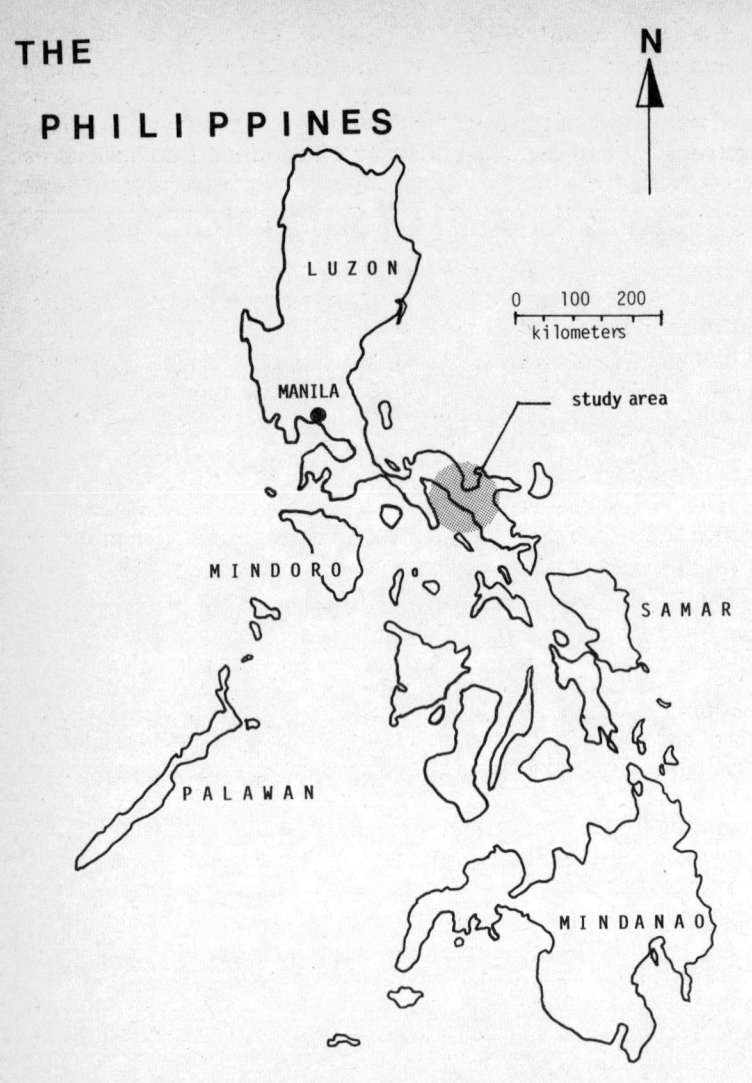

Fig. 7 *The Study Area in the Philippines*

which accounts for 30 per cent of GDP and over 50 per cent of all employment. Whilst the average income level in the Philippines is relatively high at P5,200 per capita, the distribution of this income is by no means even, with a small part of the population accounting for a large proportion of the wealth.

Farming is predominantly concerned with rice and corn for home consumption and coconuts and sugar for export. Less than half of the villages in the rural areas have direct access to roads, and movement of farm produce is initally by head-loading, animal-drawn sleds and carts. The roads to which farmers do have access are generally in poor condition. While there is an extensive system of feeder (*barangay*) roads more than 50 per cent are probably impassable during the wet season (May to November).

The study area is composed of two of the 37 municipalities comprising the Province of Camarines Sur in Southern Luzon (Figure 7). The area stretches across the Bicol Peninsula straddling the Libmanan River, the Maharlika national highway and the Philippines national railway line. The two municipalities, Libmanan and Cabusao, have a total population of 79,000 and cover an area of 38,300 ha. This implies a population density of about 200 people/sq km which is somewhat higher than the national average.

The major economic activity in the area is agriculture from which three-quarters of the population earn a living. The predominant crop is rice although coconuts, sugar cane and fish (on the coast) are of economic importance.

The area is a depressed one with a per capita income of about P1,000 compared with a national average of P5,200. Over 50 per cent of the farms are smaller than 3 ha and crop yields are low by national standards and declining. Rice production is dependent on rain-fed irrigation, and consequently only one crop is grown per year. Moreover, the majority of the farmers are share tenants which reduces the incentive to increase production. Unemployment, at 10 per cent, is high by national standards and underemployment is estimated at 30 per cent. The general picture therefore is of an area which shows the effects, in terms of unemployment, high out-migration and low crop yields, of a general lack of attention to land reform and rural development.

The transport network in the area was also in poor condition until very recently. Many villages had no link to the road network. The lack of an adequate transport system was at least partly responsible for rice being sold as wet paddy at the farm gates for prices as much as 30 per cent lower than dried paddy, and for the restricted use of fertilizers. The major transport movements in the area took place on the 'local transport system' by head-loading, by carabao sleds and carts where the footpaths or canal dykes permitted, by improvised skates on the underutilized railway lines, and by boats on the Bicol River.

The length of the road network has been extended by 50 per cent from 130 to 200 km in the last five years. The extension has been over the whole range of road types from earth feeder roads to bitumen main roads. It has increased accessibility to large towns outside the area, improved access between the two main towns, Libmanan and Cabusao, and provided road access to villages where it did not exist before.

The increase in road access has had important repercussions. It is still too early to say whether cropping patterns and agricultural output have been influenced by these improvements to the road network.[1] However, there has been a large increase in registered vehicles and traffic movements. Between 1975 and 1980 the number of buses increased by 36 per cent, jeepneys by 39 per cent and trimobiles by 57 per cent, and two new bus lines opened.

Thus, with improvement to the road system the use of motorized transport has increased. To some extent the motorized forms of transport have been brought into competition with the traditional modes. However, the most common motorized modes, jeepneys and trimobiles, are not standard western models but products of Philippine ingenuity like the skates and carabao sleds. There are estimated to be 25-30 jeepneys, 150 trimobiles and 70-100 skates operating in the study area. The numbers of carabao sleds are unknown.

Jeepneys

The jeepneys (Plate 8) evolved from experience with army surplus jeeps after the Second World War. Jeepneys have an extended chassis with a rear passenger compartment. There is a single entrance for passengers at the back and two parallel upholstered benches or seats, plus a side entrance into the driver's compartment. Jeepneys can seat a legal maximum of 16 to 22 passengers but may accommodate as many as 10 more by using the spaces available beside the driver, in the aisles, and on the running board. The rural jeepneys in the study area usually have top load railings and small cargo bars at the rear near the running board so that they can carry freight as well as passengers. Jeepneys are available with petrol or diesel engines ranging from 60-90 hp. The body and passenger compartment of a jeepney are manufactured locally, while the engine and transmission are imported. Some constructors make their own chassis while others use the chassis from a small utility truck. There are no jeepney manufacturers in the study area, although some automotive and welding shops undertake jeepney repairs and servicing.

Six jeepney operators, all using diesel-engined vehicles, were interviewed for the study. The vehicles had been purchased by their owners between 1974 and 1980, at prices ranging from P36,000 to P42,000 for new vehicles and P30,000 for one second-hand jeepney bought in 1980. The acquisition of the vehicles also entailed registration, insurance and other fees amounting to P1,000-P1,200 per jeepney. The vehicles were paid for partly in cash and partly in instalments over periods ranging from 90 days to 22 months. Down-payments to the manufacturers were made from savings, current incomes, and personal loans. The current minimum price for a new vehicle is P55,000. A down-payment of 40 per cent is normally required, and credit is available to finance purchase from banks or financing companies, although it is becoming more difficult to obtain because of re-payment problems experienced by the institutions.

Of the six informants interviewed, four drove jeepneys owned by other people, one owned two jeepneys and drove one himself, and one owned two jeepneys and employed drivers.

The respondents' jeepneys are in service for 11 to 12 hours a day, starting at 5.00 or 6.00 a.m., and some of them operate seven days a week. Each jeepney has a conductor, and a relief driver for shift work and to allow the main driver to take days off. A driver makes a total of 2 to 3 round-trips (12-18 kms per round trip) during slack or rainy days, and 3 to 5 round-trips during peak periods. Waiting times may vary from 10 to 25 minutes, depending on the level of passenger traffic. A despatcher at each of the two jeepney terminals in the Libmanan city centre controls parking and departures, and collects a terminal fee of P3 to P5 a day per vehicle.

The legal passenger fare for jeepneys is a minimum charge of PO.65, plus PO.13 for every kilometre after the first five. There is a special student rate of PO.50/first 5 km and PO.11/km thereafter. Fares, which have increased with oil prices during the last few years, vary widely according to local practices, and may exceed the legal rates.

There is no additional charge for small baskets or bundles of goods carried by jeepney passengers. However, charges are imposed when cargo attains some minimum size or bulk, or when jeepneys are on cargo-carrying trips. Fifty kilogrammes of palay (unhusked rice) costs P1.00-P1.50 to transport within the area. When a jeepney is operating on hire a unit or 'bulk rate', mutually agreed with the user, is charged for the use of the vehicle and the driver's services. The rate is based on the distance and the load involved, though the opportunity cost rather than the load may be crucial.

The informants interviewed gave figures of P225-P260 for gross daily revenues. Another survey on different routes in 1981 indicates gross daily revenues of P200-P300. Operating costs are 35-45 per cent of revenue, the major daily expense being fuel. Jeepney drivers deduct P10 to P15 a day for operating (oil and wash) and minor maintenance costs which they assume. An allowance is also made for drivers' and conductors' expenses for food and cigarettes. The driver receives 15-25 per cent of the net daily revenue after deducting operating costs, and the conductor 10 per cent. Table 39 gives a breakdown of typical daily revenue, costs and earnings, based on data supplied by informants.

The table shows that typically a conductor earns about P15 per day, a driver about P30 per day, and an owner about P110 per day. Although the drivers may undertake minor repairs themselves, the owners are responsible for major repairs, maintenance and replacement of parts. These costs, plus insurance, registration and loan repayments (if any), must be covered from the owner's earnings. One other important cost item not specifically mentioned by the informants consists of a percentage tax and fixed tax that jeepney operators as well as other public utility owners must pay to the Bureau of Internal Revenue (BIR). The former is a 2 per cent tax on quarterly gross receipts (estimated at a minimum of P72 for

Table 39. Average Daily Revenue and Earnings

		Pesos (P)
Gross Revenue		241
Operating costs		
Fuel	65	
Oil	11	
Meals/snacks	18	94
Net revenue		147
Driver's share of net revenue		29 (20%)
Conductor's share		15 (10%)
Owner's share		103 (70%)[a]

[a] This figure overstates the apparent profitability to the owner, since from his share he must bear the depreciation cost of the vehicle. Depreciation costs, based on a 10-year life, a cost price of P40,000 and 300 working days/year, would amount to about P25 per day. Maintenance and repairs could be expected to account for another P25.

each jeepney every 3 months) while the fixed tax is a flat rate of P100 a year per operator regardless of the number of vehicles that he owns.

Based on interviews with users, jeepneys are used mostly for work-related trips, although social visits, church-going and recreation are sometimes included in trip-purposes. According to jeepney operators, the most frequent passengers are students and schoolchildren, housewives and market vendors. Farmers and government employees are less frequent jeepney passengers.

Jeepney operators perceive an increasing supply of and demand for motorized public transport. The number of jeepneys and trimobiles in the area has grown and people travel more often now than before. This appears to be a consequence of economic and road improvements in the area. However, the major constraint on the frequency of travel is cost, and attempts to increase fares have been strongly resisted. Although demand has increased, jeepney operators report declining net revenues because of growing competition in the sector, and increasing operating and maintenance costs. Compared with other modes available, the major advantages of jeepneys to users are that they are readily available, comfortable, safe, fast, and have a longer range than other modes.

The jeepney operators and drivers do not think that improved vehicle design would reduce prices. While jeepneys could be made larger, more comfortable, and more durable for rural conditions, the costs of manufacture cannot decline, mainly because the costs of materials have steadily grown.

Trimobiles

The trimobile is a local adaptation of an imported technology. It is a motorcycle modified to carry additional goods and passengers by the addition of a side-car (Plate 9). Both new and used Japanese motorcycles with engine capacities in the range of 100 to 125 cc are converted into trimobiles. The local conversion process involves modifying the motorcycle frame for attaching the side-car. The wheels are sometimes reinforced and extra shock absorbers attached to cope with rural road conditions. The side-car consists of a driver cabin, a passenger compartment with a cargo rack above it and an additional cargo rack at the rear. The side-car is of welded construction, from steel bar and sheet. The upholstered seat can accommodate 2 or 3 persons, but metal railings usually supply one or two extra seats in the passenger compartment. Additional passengers can be seated behind the driver or on the cargo rack if it is designed to allow this. The side-car wheel is of welded construction consisting of a hub, reinforced rim and steel rod spokes. Trimobiles are manufactured by local welding shops in the study area, and on a larger scale by workshops in Naga City. The motorcycle is usually purchased beforehand by the would-be trimobile owner, who then brings it for conversion to a side-car maker.

Nine trimobile operators were interviewed for the study. Most of the study respondents had acquired their trimobiles brand new for prices ranging from P8,500 to P11,000, of which the side-car accounted for P1,000 to P2,000. Registration and other fees were an additional P500 to P1,000. Other vehicles were purchased second-hand for P2,000 to P5,000. In most cases, the owners paid cash for their vehicles. In some instances, short-term credit (2-10 months) was extended by the motor-cycle dealer or the side-car manufacturer for part of the cost. In one case, the owner had borrowed part of the money from the Libmanan Rural Bank. The current minimum price of a new trimobile is about P13,000. Dealers may extend credit to a buyer themselves or arrange credit through a finance or banking institution for the purchaser of the motorcycle. The terms vary from 10-30 per cent down payment and 12-36 months repayment period. Before a buyer is extended credit, an investigation is conducted into his 'character', capacity to pay, and credit record. A comprehensive insurance policy and a chattel mortgage on the vehicle are also required. Collateral such as farmland may be required by a bank. The rural banks very rarely give loans for the purchase of trimobiles.

Of the nine informants interviewed, four drove trimobiles owned by other people, three owned one vehicle each, one owned two vehicles and one owned three. For most of the owners and drivers, the business is their primary or only source of income. Some owners drive their own vehicles, others prefer to hire their trimobiles to drivers who are related or known to them.

Trimobiles operate for 10 to 12 hours a day, starting at 6.00 or 7.00 a.m. and the use of relief drivers is unusual. Operating patterns depend on weather conditions and trip lengths, varying from 3 to 10 round trips a day.

The minimum fare per passenger is PO.6 and increases at a rate of PO.12 per km after the first 5 kilometres. Road conditions are also considered, so that a trip on bad roads to a nearby destination may cost more than a trip on better roads to a more distant place. Cargo fares also vary depending on the kind and quantity of goods carried and the distance travelled. A sack of palay or a bag of fertilizer may cost only the minimum, but fares are greater for remote destinations, e.g. P1.00-P1.50 for 50 kg of palay or rice. As many as 10 bags of fertilizer or 350-500 kg of palay can be loaded on a trimobile if no passengers other than the cargo owner are on board.

Unlike the jeepney drivers in the area, who get a commission, the trimobile drivers pay a daily 'boundary' or fixed rental to the owners for the use of their vehicles and receive the revenue left over after other daily expenses, including those for fuel, have been met. The gross revenues reported by the trimobile owners and drivers are considerably lower than those reported by jeepney operators and drivers, but their net average revenues are about the same at P26 per day. A typical boundary fee is P17, and running costs average about P19 per day, with fuel taking up at least 75 per cent of the total[2]. From his earnings the owner has to bear the cost of maintenance and spare parts, insurance, registration and depreciation. Trimobile operators are liable to a 2 per cent tax on gross income and a fixed tax of P100 per year, but the Bureau of Internal Revenue experiences difficulties in trying to collect these taxes.

Trimobiles are used mostly for work-related trips — students, school children, farmers and housewives being the most frequent passengers. The predominance of these three groups probably reflects the primarily local clientele of trimobiles. With the new or improved roads, trimobiles have penetrated more isolated areas, enabling their local residents to travel more often by road rather than by railway skate or waterway and to bring goods to or from the market by motor vehicle rather than by head porterage or animal-drawn vehicle. In turn, groups from the cities and outside are better able to visit the peripheral communities. These include midwives, teachers, and other government field personnel with no service vehicles. The major advantages of trimobiles are that they can go to places inaccessible to jeepneys and bring passengers much closer to their destinations.

Trimobile owners and driver-respondents generally share the views of the jeepney operators and drivers about the increasing number of vehicles, frequency of travel by people in the area, economic and road improvements, and growing patronage of trimobiles. According to them, travel and economic life have only improved for some parts of the population. Some roads are still rough and impassable during the rains, and trimobiles are used for internal travel because there are no other alternatives.

The trimobile owners and drivers complain about stagnant or declining levels of patronage and revenues due to growing competition and operating costs. Trimobile driving alone does not provide an adequate income, especially to support a big family, unless a driver manages to acquire a trimobile of his own. However, there is a general optimism about the future of the business as economic development increases the demand for travel.

Skates

Skates (Plate 10) are used for transporting people and freight on the under-utilized railway lines. A skate is a simple device usually made by the owner, sometimes with the help of a carpenter. It consists of a wooden frame, a bamboo floor, one to four wooden benches on the platform but no roof, and pairs of ball-bearing wheels placed just wide enough apart to fit the railway track. To keep the skate on the track and to minimize friction while the vehicle is in operation, two additional pairs of smaller ball-bearing wheels are installed underneath so that they roll against the side of each rail, and the driver lubricates the wheels with oil every so often. A skate is propelled by foot by the driver, often with the help of an assistant or one of the passengers. A wooden pedal with a rubber pad is tilted down against the rail to slow down or stop the skate.

Although it does not attain great speed, a skate can gain momentum with a heavy load. Otherwise, it is light enough to be carried by a man or two boys so that it can be turned around, 'parked' off the track when not in service or, as often happens, quickly unloaded and carried off the track when the train comes. A bigger skate may be propelled by a small engine (e.g. a 5 hp rice thresher motor) attached to the floor at the rear and connected to one of the rear wheels by a fan belt. These wheels have a larger circumference, and one is thicker to accommodate the belt. An additional foot lever serves to regulate the speed of the vehicle by tightening or relaxing the fan belt as the motor operates. A manual skate seats five to eight persons but can carry as many as a dozen, while a motorized skate with four benches can seat 22 and carry a maximum of 25 passengers. A manual skate may carry as much as 750 kg of palay on a single cargo trip, and a motorized skate can manage 1,500 kg.

Four skate operators, one of whom had a motorized version, were interviewed for the study. All four were owners who drove their own skates but all regarded this as a secondary source of income, their main jobs being farming. The owner of the motorized skate used his engine to drive his rice thresher at harvest time. The operators had built their skates partly to meet their own transport needs as well as for public use. A manual skate costs about P100, and a motorized version up to P2,000.

Skate drivers work 11 to 12 hours a day but are mostly active during the early morning and late afternoon. They normally wait for a full load at the railway station, and unload and pick up passengers along the journey. Skates average 3-4 round trips per day but when demand is high can make up to 6-8 trips. The data obtained from respondents cannot be converted meaningfully into fare rates per passenger/km. For longer journeys, rates appear to be approximately P0.15/km, but are probably higher for short trips. A study of South Luzon [3] in 1981 estimated rates at P0.25/km. Freight rates are based on equivalent passenger space occupied. The skate is not generally claimed to be cheaper than other means of transport.

Operating and maintenance expenses of manual skates are small at about P2 per day. Daily revenues from skate operations appear to be equally low. Daily net earnings range from P7 (single-bench) to P20 (including the motorized skate); gross earnings range from P10 (manual) to P40 (motorized).

Skate-driving does not appear to offer good prospects as a source of income unless it is regarded as a secondary occupation and/or combined with private use. Estimates of the number of skates in the study area vary from 70 to 100, and there is no clear evidence of trends in demand. The skate appears to have certain disadvantages. It is not a fast means of transport, nor is it convenient. Since it has no canopy, the passengers are exposed to sun and wind — no skate runs when it is raining. When two skates meet travelling in opposite directions along the single track, one must yield. There is the obvious safety hazard of having to clear the skate and passengers from the track when a train approaches. However, skates are used by various groups of people, farmers, school children, market vendors and teachers being the most frequent passengers according to the respondents.

The demand for skates may be limited to those living in or having to do with railroad communities that remain inaccessible to road transport, but it is a flexible demand. Skates are easy enough to make and operate, and the investment required is relatively low, so that questions of skills or credit do not appear to be salient in decisions to enter this field, unless a motorized skate is contemplated. Formal regulations on skates are virtually non-existent. Currently, there seems to be grudging official acknowledgement of their necessity for railroad villages.

Carabao sleds

Carabaos are used in the study area for farming. Sleds or wheeled carts are used by carabao owners for transport purposes. The prevailing price of a carabao is about P1,200, but a bigger and healthier one may cost up to P2,000. However, for farmers who own carabaos, a sled provides a means of transport at minimal additional cost. The sled (Plate 11) consists of a flat bed of bamboo strips and wood frame nailed to a pair of bamboo poles, which are attached to another pair of poles harnessed to the yoke on the carabao. The ends of the poles touching the ground serve as the runners, the harness pair moving freely on wooden hinges for turning purposes. The sled is very simple to make and materials are available from bamboo clumps and young trees nearby. The only purchased items required for the sled itself are a length of rope and nails. The wooden yoke, which is also used for the agricultural implements drawn by the carabao, is available ready-made in the market for about P12.

The maintenance cost of the sled appears to be low. The wooden runners wear quickly where they drag on the ground and are repaired or replaced once a week on average, but the rope is replaced only once a year and the yoke may last up to five years.

The sled is used to transport various kinds of farm products, materials, and household needs over short distances on or off the road. Passengers may also be ferried, although the particular design described above is not very suitable for this purpose. (Elsewhere in the country, such as in Central Luzon provinces, the sled is built so that passengers can ride more comfortably. The bed is level and built higher above the ground, and the runners are flat on the ground rather than slanting on their heels.)

Two carabao sled owners were interviewed. In one case, the owner is a share tenant on a coconut farm and uses the sled for his family's transport needs. It is also rented to other farmers to carry their copra, palay and firewood. The rental rate is approximately P2.5 per 100 kg per km. The other informant is a rice farmer and uses his sled exclusively to transport his own palay.

Carabao sleds were used extensively for freight transport in the past, but their numbers have declined in recent years. The number of carabaos also appears to have declined and there is some evidence of the increasing use of power tillers in the study area. As a result of road improvements and the growth of motor transport, carabao sleds now appear to be used mainly in coastal, hilly and other areas not yet accessible by road. However, they can still be observed from time to time on roads in the study area, even along the highway. The utility of the carabao sled on and around the farm suggests that it will probably continue to be used for on-farm transport.

Plate 9 *A passenger carrying trimobile*

Plate 10 *Foot propelled Skate with typical passenger load*

Plate 11 *Carabao Sled Carrying bags of fertilizer along a track*

Plate 12 *The predominant means of transport in Makete District*

Comparison of means of transport

The analysis of the four different means offers some interesting comparisons, a summary of which is presented in Table 40.
 In some way, the four means complement each other in their operations and serve the various transport needs of a rural and agricultural community that is still developing internal and external linkages. The jeepneys provide inter-town service for small merchants, farmers, students, employees, and bulk cargo. The trimobiles cater for the intra-town journeys of housewives, market-goers, farmers and school children, especially between the Libmanan town centre and outlying areas. The skates and sleds serve the transport needs of the settlements and farms off the road network. Except for the sled, which is associated with farm work, these modes appear to serve an equally wide variety of clientele and trip-purposes, with farm-to-market journeys as a common denominator. Thus, over time, they have also tended to compete and with the improvements of road links, the jeepneys and trimobiles, which offer a more convenient, faster and wide-ranging means of moving goods and people, have gained ground on the traditional modes. Skates remain a necessary means of transport for railroad-linked communities and sleds are still useful at least as a private vehicle on the farm.
 Their salient characteristics invite comparisons between the jeepneys and trimobiles on the one hand, and the skates and sleds on the other. Both motorized, the jeepneys and trimobiles are built and maintained by skilled workers, automotive shops, and supporting enterprises. They are 'operated' (in the legal sense) by owners who are often distinct from the vehicle drivers. Their acquisition, operating and maintenance costs are substantial, and require some form of purchase financing. Since they are for public use, their manufacture, acquisition, and operation are subject to government regulation, although their current legal status is hazy. Table 40 shows that their charges, for passengers and freight, are very similar.
 Due to the greater degree of specialization and scale required in their manufacture, marketing, operation and regulation, these modes employ more skilled workers, operators (including distinct 'professional drivers'), entrepreneurs and managers than the skates and sleds do. Between the two motorized modes, the technically more demanding jeepney generates more jobs and income per vehicle than the trimobile does. However, the trimobile appears to have greater potential for local manufacturing, servicing and maintenance activities. There are fewer jeepney-building

Table 40. Transport Mode Comparison

Mode	Purchase Price (p)	Potential load	Hire charges (P) Passenger	Hire charges (P) Freight[1]	Daily income (P) Driver	Daily income (P) Owner
Jeepney	56,000	20-25 passengers	0.13/km	2-4 per tonne/km	20-30	100-110
Trimobile	13,500	5-6 passengers or 450 kg	0.12/km	1.5-3.0 per tonne/km	20-35	15-20
Skate Manual	100	5-8 passengers or 750 kg	0.15-0.25/km	3-6 per tonne/km	7-20	—
Skate Motorized	1,750	20-25 passengers or 1,500 kg	0.15-0.25/km	3-6 per tonne/km	7-20	—
Sled	15	—	—	25 per tonne/km	—	—

[1] These figures are interpreted from the study data and should be treated with caution since freight is not usually charged at a rate per kg but on the basis of space occupied or per sack. Rates vary according to route, road condition and distance.

shops and they are confined to Naga City or more remote urban centres, though they serve and depend on a larger market. There are more trimobile shops and a few have been set up in Libmanan. In terms of equipment, capital and skill requirements it is easier and less costly for local shops to extend their activities into trimobile-making than jeepney-building. They also have the incentive of a larger demand for new trimobiles, repair and rehabilitation which ensures a larger volume of work.

Thus, what the trimobiles lack in terms of job-creating capacity per vehicle they compensate for with their greater numbers in the locality where they operate. For example, while they have not hired conductors or despatchers, trimobiles have employed more operators and drivers, many of whom may have no job options. Similarly, what they lack in individual carrying capacity and operating range the trimobiles make up for with their ability to penetrate peripheral or interstitial rural communities less accessible to jeepneys.

Skates and sleds are much easier and cheaper to build and operate. Their manufacture and operation are well within local control in terms of existing skills, resources, and infrastructure. However, they generate not only fewer jobs, but also fewer full-time, permanent ones than jeepneys and trimobiles do, and are more subject to the vicissitudes of weather, demand and operators with other primary occupations. The service that the skates and sleds provide is on the whole more limited in scope, and is more likely to be for personal use than in the case of the two other modes.

Household income seems to be a crucial factor in the demand for the acquisition of jeepneys and trimobiles. Because the vehicles are expensive both current income, accrued savings and physical or commercial assets are important. Formal or informal credit may be required to supplement current income for the lumpy investment involved in jeepney or trimobile purchase and amortization. The institutional credit framework is a constraint on vehicle purchases. While trimobile makers extend short-term credit at no interest, this tends to tie down their usually limited working capital. Motor-cycle dealers and financing institutions provide credit, but at high interest rates, and require credit checks and collateral. The latter is usually the vehicle itself but may have to be farm land or a house if the borrower makes no down payment. The risk of foreclosure may be a strong disincentive in a rural setting where land is a precious possession and where share tenancy still seems to prevail despite its official disappearance.

Summary

This study is the only one to focus on for hire and reward transport services. It illustrates the evolution of these services in an area that has undergone significant changes in the scale and pattern of transport. The advancement of the motorized modes at the expense of skates and sleds is what might be expected. However it is noteworthy that the sled, a very simple but useful means of load carrying, remains important for private use by farmers. Of greater significance is the role played by the trimobile which, with its low capital cost and operational flexibility, offers a more extensive and dispersed service than the more conventional motor vehicle, the jeepney, but at competitive charges.

PART III — TRANSPORT POLICIES

CHAPTER 8

Transport in a Rural Community in Tanzania[†]

Introduction

The Ukinga area of Tanzania forms part of the Makete District which lies in the west of Tanzania. It is an isolated region and efforts to assist its development have been evidently hampered by the lack of transport. The terrain makes any kind of movement slow and expensive. Moreover, in a broader sense, Ukinga is located in a country beset by economic crises not least of which has been the escalating price of oil.

The study was initiated by a non-governmental organization. In defining measures to improve the transport system in the areas, they insisted on a low level approach using local resources. This type of approach they felt could be replicable and sustainable. They stressed the need to include all travel needs and the consideration of 'track' and 'vehicle' requirements as mutually dependent parts of the transport system.

The study, therefore, was more concerned with developing an approach to transport based on a qualitative assessment of the relationship between transport and development. It was carried out in 1981 by Ian Barwell and John Howe of Intermediate Technology Transport Ltd. Since the time of the study the Ukinga area has been formally integrated into the newly formed Makete District.

Background

The approach to the study was constrained by the fact that the field work had to be completed within a period of three weeks. It

---

[†]This chapter is based on a study carried out by I. Barwell and J. Howe for the Christian Council of Tanzania. At the time of the study T.Sh.9.2 (Tanzanian Shillings) = US$1.0.

was conditioned by the emphasis on identifying priorities for improvement to the transport system which were sensitive to the requirements of the local people, could be implemented and sustained at low-cost using local resources, and would complement improvements likely to be implemented by the Government.

The field survey therefore focused on:

1 a route characteristics inventory of the roads and tracks in the area;
2 information collection interviews with village groups, church and party representatives in most of the villages in the area;
3 discussions with many government, party, church, medical, education and other community representatives about the nature — magnitude, frequency, type of vehicle or other mode used — of travel needs and difficulties, and to cross-check information on the location of facilities, development prospects and priorities, and attitudes towards community-based initiatives.

The study area

Ukinga is an area in the Livingstone Mountains lying along the south-western border of Tanzania (Figure 8) adjacent to the northernmost shores of Lake Malawi. It lies to the south of the main trunk road — connecting Dar-es-Salaam to Mbeya and the Zambia border — from which it is separated by the almost sheer slope of the Rift Valley. A similar escarpment separates Ukinga from the fertile flat lands on the northern shores of Lake Malawi. On its north-eastern and eastern sides Ukinga merges slowly into the lower, flatter lands of the Njombe area.

Ukinga has a population of some 91,000. In accordance with the nation's policy of *ujamaa*, the vast majority of these people live in villages rather than in scattered houses. This means that there are often wide tracts of empty lands between villages. The population of Ukinga has been growing only very slowly, and much less than the national average of 2.6 per cent per annum. This is because of emigration of the young and the men from the area. The people of Ukinga have a good reputation as hard workers and find it reasonably easy to get work in other regional centres. One of the reasons for initiating the study was to try to accelerate economic and social development so as to put a brake on this process. There are no major towns in Ukinga and the whole of the population can be described as rural. The main population centres tend to be situated along the Njombe-Bulongwa road and include Tandala, Iwawa

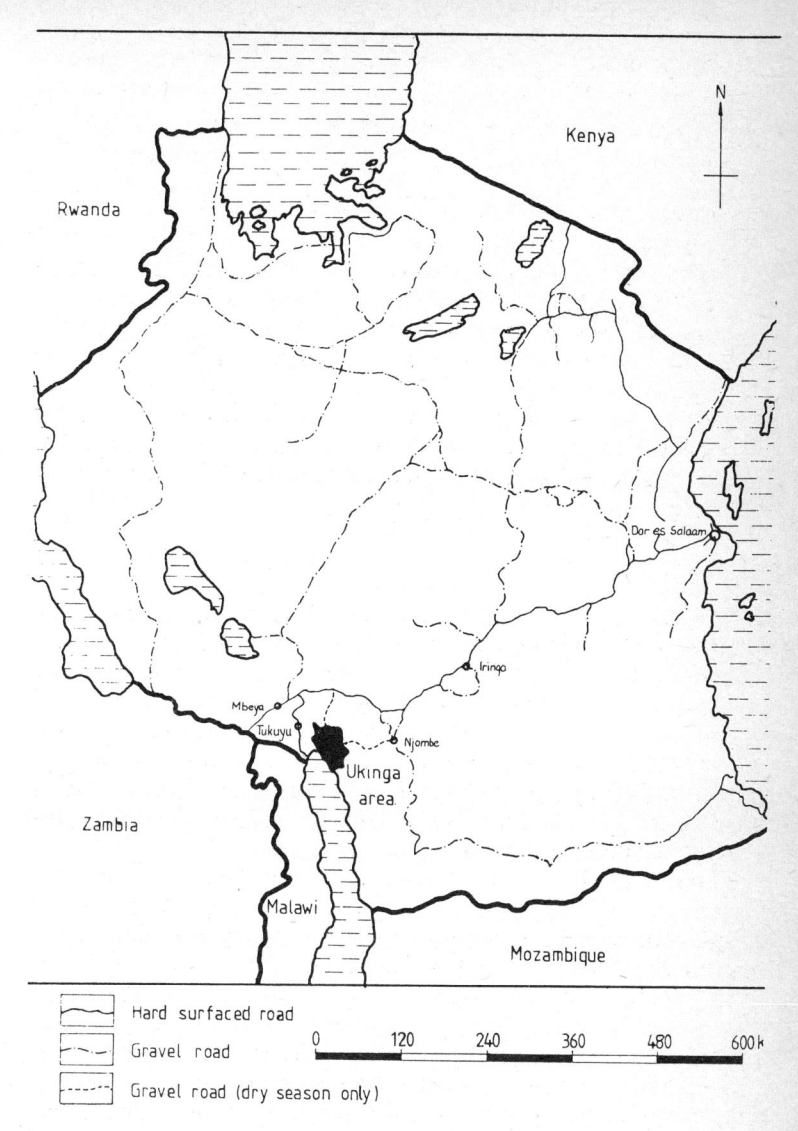

Fig. 8 *Tanzania*

and Bulongwa itself (Figure 9). There are hospitals near Tandala and Bulongwa.

Administratively Ukinga falls within the District of Makete which, in turn, is a part of Iringa Region. Ukinga is at the extreme western edge of the region and in the past has suffered by virtue of its location. Until 1979 it was part of Njombe District but in an attempt to speed up development and direct resources to Ukinga the separate District of Makete has been created, the headquarters of which are located at Iwawa.

The altitude of Ukinga, which varies from 1,500-2,200 metres above sea level (with the highest parts in the west, overlooking the Rift Valley) is a major determinant of the climate. The high temperatures which would be expected by virtue of its location at about 9° south of the Equator are modified to such an extent that Ukinga has a climate very similar to that of the world's temperate zones.

The long period of rainfall from November to May means that the predominantly earth-surfaced roads are often impassable for six months of the year. The muddy roads caused by the long rainy period (the rain tends to fall steadily over extended periods, rather than as short, sharp tropical rainstorms) are a major communications problem. It is extremely difficult for vehicles to pass unless they have 4-wheel-drive; it is, of course, equally difficult to use simple vehicles such as bicycles or handcarts.

Social and economic aspects

Ukinga's location caused it to be neglected by earlier authorities and this is reflected in the lack of facilities and infrastructure. There is nowhere locally to obtain capital equipment, spare parts or administrative material. Such items may be obtained either in Njombe or Iringa (about 300 km away).

Government facilities are being expanded but it will be some years before they are fully operational and able to play a dominant role in the development of the District. Private sector facilities are minimal. There are few shops or other services and only the most basic commodities can be bought. Crucially, there are no garages with repair facilities or fuel supplies, although the Government plans to build one to meet its own requirements and to provide a limited service to the private sector so as to cover running costs. The contribution of the church to development infrastructure — in the form of medical facilities, shops, mills and water and electricity projects, etc. — is important and likely to remain so.

Ukinga's lack of development infrastructure is exacerbated by its remoteness and the difficulty of any form of communication

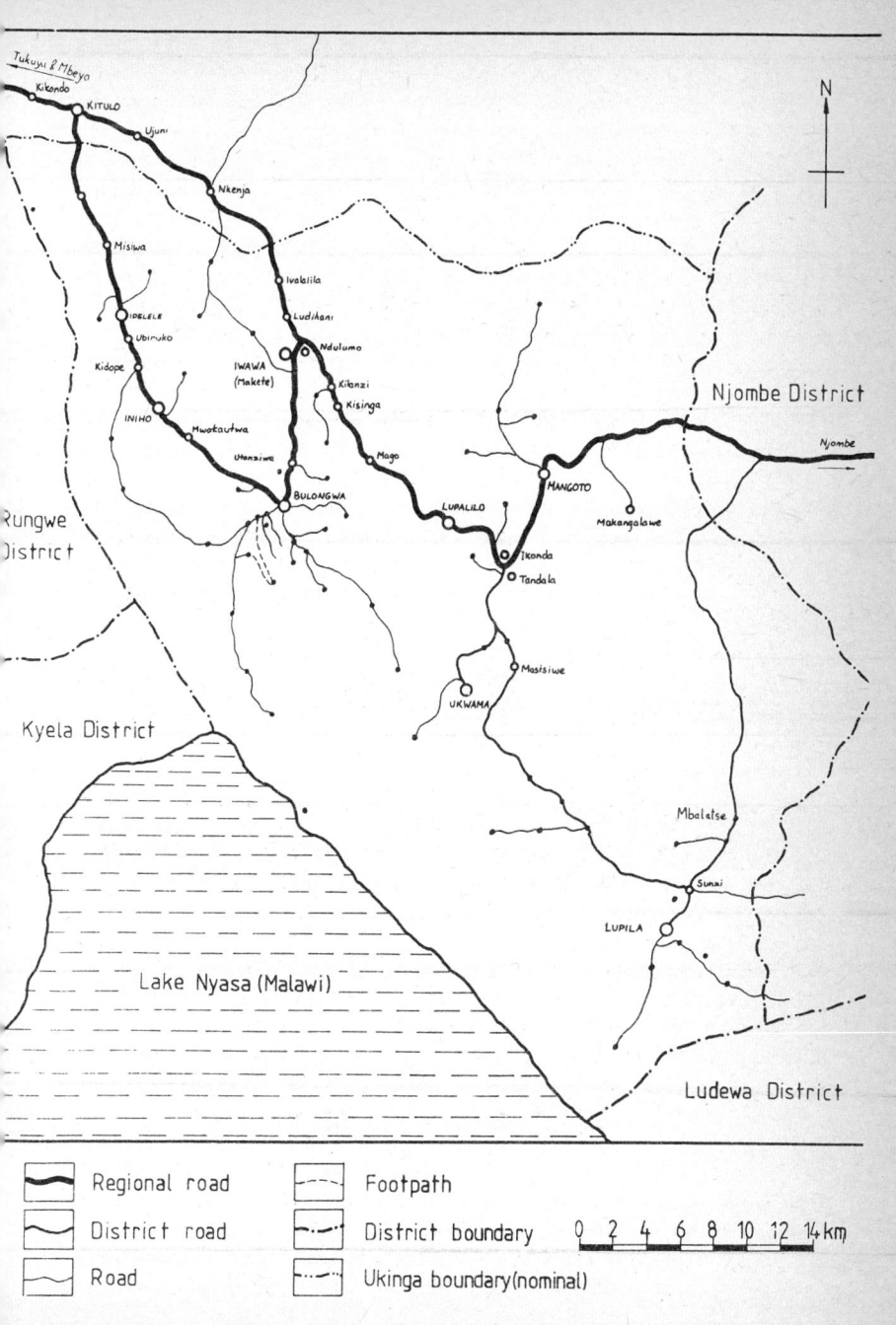

Fig. 9 *Ukinga Area (Makete District)*

with the outside world and within the District. It is about 100 km to Njombe — the former district centre which offers better private sector services than those available within Ukinga — by a predominantly dry season road. Bus services from Njombe to Ukinga are suspended in the wet season. Mbeya, the nearest regional centre, is about 90 km away, but the road is of a poorer standard than that to Njombe and there is no bus service at all. It is noteworthy that all manufactured goods, particularly building materials, have to come into Ukinga via the Njombe/Mbeya connections.

The Ukinga area does not have a telephone service and communication from Makete District to other parts of Tanzania is via the police radio network and limited to emergencies only. The effect of poor communications within the District is most evident in the concern of villages about access to hospital facilities at Bulongwa and Tandala. This consistently emerges as one of their major reasons for wishing to improve transport services. The mobile clinics are highly regarded and undoubtedly do valuable work, but the number of places served is limited and the service is frequently disrupted by the state of the road network. Villagers are forcible in expressing their need of quick access to a hospital in emergency situations.

The counterpart to Ukinga's lack of development infrastructure and remoteness is that it is an area of considerable economic potential. Because of its geography, the fertility of its soil and the hard-working and enterprising nature of its people, a wide range of temperate and tropical produce can be grown; the area is also suitable for sheep and cattle farming with associated wool and dairying activities. Pyrethrum is the only major cash commodity being actively developed. Under a World Bank project[1] improvements are to be carried out to about 50 km of Regional road and 10 km of District road in Northern Ukinga. The Tanganyika Pyrethrum Board (TPB) is to be provided with twelve 7-tonne trucks for transport from buying centres to main stores; five 4-wheel-drive station wagons to reach villages inaccessible by truck; and 21 motor cycles for TPB field staff.

There is said to be considerable scope for coffee in the areas aroung Ipelele, and some villages in the centre and extreme south of Ukinga. The first would benefit from the route improvements to be carried out on behalf of the TPB.

There is considerable scope for the export of food crops, but obstacles to this are typified by those with fruit and potatoes. The Ukinga area could produce considerable quantities of temperate fruits: apples, pears, peaches, etc. These are obviously perishable and easily damaged, and the harvest period coincides with the rainy seasons when travel is most difficult. Proposals for a fruit cannery have been discussed but the difficulty is that, given the absence of other commodities suitable for canning, the plant will be idle most of the year rendering the investment uneconomic. Potatoes could also be grown on a large scale but, given their bulk and low value, they require a sophisticated marketing and transport system if they are to be exploited successfully.

Another feature of the agricultural economy is the role played by the villages in the south-west of Ukinga close to the escarpment. They are centres for the trade, via the escarpment of the Livingstone Mountains, with the villages of the Lake Malawi plain and Kyela District. Ukinga obtains rice, bananas, sugar cane, cassava, ground nuts, oranges and fish via Tukuyu. In return it trades wheat, potatoes, peas, beans, cow and dairy products. All of this trade is on foot with headloading as the only means of goods carriage.

The last feature of Ukinga's economy worthy of note is the range of skills to be found in such activities as carpentry, basket weaving and hoe handle and grass slasher manufacture, etc.

Transport in Ukinga

Very little of the economic potential of Ukinga is realized, to the detriment of its people and of Tanzania, since the area could make a contribution to reducing the country's existing food deficit. Undoubtedly, a major reason for this situation is the extremely poor state of Ukinga's transport system. It also greatly limits the extent and frequency of welfare and other services. Essentially there are two main problems: the scarcity of vehicles and the poor conditions of the roads.

Vehicles
With the exception of the limited deliveries to the regional and district trading shops, pyrethrum collections by the TPB, and the bus services from Njombe[2] which operate only in the dry season, Ukinga does not have any organized passenger or goods distribution services. The hiring of, or visits by, commercial vehicles from outside of Makete District are rare events. There are no locally owned and operated motor vehicle services available to the public except for those provided informally, and on a very limited basis, by the church. Because of the tough road conditions traders from outside Makete are unwilling to penetrate the area. Local vehicle ownership is virtually non-existent and appears constrained by a

combination of factors additional to the poor road conditions and lack of repair facilities and fuel supplies. Among these are the national shortage of motor vehicles, the difficulty of raising the necessary foreign exchange and the locally depressed economic conditions.

Motor vehicle imports are controlled by the State Motor Corporation and allocated to each Region by the central government. An allocation committee, under the Regional Development Director (RDD), decides the distribution of vehicles within each Region. The Iringa RDD stated that at the last meeting of his committee there were 300 applications for 35 vehicles. One of these vehicles was allocated to an individual from Makete because of the rarity of applications from the District and because it was felt that he would 'serve the people'.

Theoretically, the Government will give priority and assistance to the application of village groups for a vehicle, providing the villagers have first raised a proportion of the money required. In practice few seem able to do this because of the difficulty of turning surplus produce into cash.[3] Headloading and walking are the main means of movement. Journeys by these means to Tukuyu ($1\frac{1}{2}$ days), Mbeye (2-$2\frac{1}{2}$ days) and Njombe ($2\frac{1}{2}$-3 days) for special supplies, such as building materials, and to sell produce are not uncommon. Bicycle, handcart and wheelbarrow ownership are rare so movements around the farm and within the village also rely on headloading and walking (Plate 12).

Roads
The Regional, District, and Village road systems are as depicted in Figure 9. Whilst the alignment of most of the Regional road system is of a reasonable standard given the terrain, the surfacing renders travel difficult in the rainy season. The Regional class road from Bulongwa to Kitulo via Ipelele, and most of the District road system, is in a barely motorable condition and travel is slow, dangerous and very costly. Most of the surface is seriously eroded and much of the alignment substandard, being tortuous, narrow and with sections of gradient in excess of 15 per cent. This group of roads requires major engineering to re-align substandard sections and reconstruct the formation: drains, culverts and bridges also required reinstatement. The Village road system has been constructed almost entirely by voluntary labour and is a significant testimonial to the determination and enterprise of the Ukinga people. Notwithstanding this, the system is in poor condition. The roads have not been built according to basic engineering principles and few have any positive drainage. Many are narrow and unac-

ceptably steep. Most are unsurfaced and eroded (Plates 13, 14 and 15).

The lack of vehicles combined with the poor condition of the roads contributes significantly to Ukinga's social and economic problems. Church, health and school programmes are maintained only at great difficulty and expense, and services cannot be extended to all those that require them. Fruit rots on the trees and potatoes in the ground and stores. Many people are discouraged from producing more by the certain knowledge that the surplus cannot be sold.

Whilst it is considered important not to overemphasize the benefits, social and economic, that could be expected from improvements in Ukinga's transport, they are none the less real and it appears unlikely that they could be achieved by other means. It is possible to envisage non-transport ways of overcoming some of the current demands for movement, but they cannot be eliminated: some examples illustrate this.

The water supply project at Utengule will minimize personal movements associated with obtaining water for household and other community needs in the village. However, diesel fuel for the pumps will have to be brought in from Iwawa and headloaded down a steep valley to the pumping station. All building supplies for the project have been headloaded a distance of 8 km. In a similar way, the creation of more village health centres might reduce the need for the services of the mobile clinics. However, supplies would have to be delivered to the centres and seriously ill people will still need access to hospital. The latter will require adequate roads and vehicles to use them. More generally, a simple telecommunications network could greatly reduce the need for personal travel. Action in this sector is clearly a government prerogative and with all Makete's other development needs such a network seems unlikely to materialize for some years to come.

Improvements to the transport system in Ukinga

The deficiencies in Ukinga's transport are such that movement needs are only likely to be satisfied by a package of improvements.

Essentially, four types of improvement are desirable:

1 Encourage the use of low-cost vehicles for the movement of loads around the village (firewood, water, manure, building materials, etc.) and, where appropriate, of produce to market. This will:

- allow substantially larger loads to be moved, compared with headloading, reduce the time and effort involved and stimulate marketing within the District;
- improve employment since there is potential within Ukinga for the use and local manufacture of several such vehicles.

2 Stimulate the local ownership and operation of goods/passenger-carrying motor vehicles. This will:
- assist the people of Ukinga to move their crops to the profitable markets of Mbeya and Njombe;
- improve personal mobility;
- assist the import of essential goods (e.g. building materials) into the District;
- improve access to local facilities.

3 Upgrade District and Regional class roads to improve all-year-round access. This will:
- permit all-year-round passenger and goods access from Njombe and Mbeya to the major centres of Ukinga;
- improve access for government, church, party and medical vehicles between major centres of Ukinga.

4 Upgrade Village class roads to improve all-year-round access. This will:
- improve access to government, party and church organizations and to medical facilities;
- in conjunction with 2, assist in movement of crops to profitable markets.

The four improvements are inter-related and to effect some and not others would reduce the benefits that could be expected. For example, the upgrading of a village road alone will be unlikely to have economic benefits unless the connection to a focus of activity is direct, or via District/Regional roads offering a similar level of access.

The benefits of locally owned and operated motor vehicles will obviously be greater if they are introduced together with improved feeder and main roads. (At present the benefits of locally owned motor vehicles are limited by the fact that access to many places is difficult or impossible in wet weather and because vehicle operating costs are high.) If Regional roads are improved, traders from surrounding Districts might travel into Ukinga to buy produce; the use of local vehicles will ensure:

- control over the marketing of produce, particularly its timing;
- that the profits from marketing are retained in the area;

— the availability of transport for the import of goods and for local welfare and social purposes.

The present District administration is young and still lacking essential facilities, services, personnel, materials and equipment. Because of financial and resource constraints, the role of the Regional and District authorities in implementing these improvements is likely to be limited to upgrading of the Regional and District class roads. The recurrent budget and resources available to the District Works Engineer are inadequate for other than limited maintenance to the District class road system.

Low-cost vehicles

The particular conditions of the Ukinga area — terrain, smallholder-based agriculture giving rise to relatively small consignment sizes, inadequacy of the transport system and the expense of providing for extensive movement by motor vehicle — make it a very suitable location for the use of low-cost vehicles. A great deal of time and effort is devoted to transport, especially if household requirements are taken into consideration. The most basic movement demands are the carriage of water and firewood to the village, sometimes from considerable distances and frequently over steep or broken terrain. Farmed land is often remote from the village and both inputs and outputs have to be moved between them. Cargoes are headloaded long distances up and down the escarpment; from Ukinga to Tukuyu, Mbeya and Njombe; and from the villages to major markets in Makete. Whatever is done to improve the road system and to make motor vehicles more widely available, it is apparent that much transport will continue to take place on the tracks and footpaths that criss-cross Ukinga.

Given the effort the people are prepared to put into carrying loads on their heads, there is potential for introducing non-mechanized vehicles to utilize this effort more efficiently and to reduce the time and the arduousness of this transport element. Since we are primarily concerned with low-cost vehicles for own-use by the poor, then cost, scarcity of fuel, complexity and the difficulty of obtaining spare parts all argue against mechanized transport. The existing use of non-mechanized vehicles in Ukinga supports this approach. Even in mountainous villages several bicycles are found in use. Whilst such a vehicle is not well suited to the terrain and few journeys can be accomplished without pushing the bicycle part of the way, its use clearly indicates that it is regarded by the people themselves as better than the alternatives: walking or headloading. Similarly, isolated examples of crude wheelbarrows of all-wood construction are seen in Ukinga. Again their use, however inefficient, indicates they are preferred to the alternatives of human carriage. Neither bicycles nor efficient wheelbarrows are readily available in Njombe, Mbeya or Iringa, much less in Ukinga.

The use of animals removes, or reduces considerably, the human effort required to move loads. Substantial loads can be moved even across difficult terrain. It would be feasible for two persons to control a train of ten or more pack-carrying donkeys on any of the trading routes traversing the escarpment separating Ukinga from the Lake Malawi communities. Such a train could move substantially more than the humans involved: each animal, depending on breed and condition being capable of moving 3 to 6 times the weight to be carried by a human. The people of Ukinga are used to dealing with animals, but not with work animals, so a learning process would be involved in their introduction.

It is considered that there is potential within Ukinga for the use of several types of low-cost vehicles:

— *chee-geh* and shoulder pole;
— wheelbarrows and handcarts;
— animal transport (sledge, pack animal and cart);
— cycle panniers and trailers (including those for evacuating patients to hospital in the absence of motor transport).

Most of these vehicles could be manufactured locally, and indeed should be to ensure availability.

Local operation of motor vehicles

There are in Ukinga no locally owned and operated vehicles whose services the public can use. The reported hiring, by individuals in Ukinga, of vehicles from Njombe or Mbeya is unattractive because of the difficulty of arranging cargo in both directions with consequent increased hire costs. To overcome the difficulties this situation imposes, the introduction of a pilot vehicle hire scheme is proposed. This has both long and short-term objectives:

1 *long-term* — to improve the access of villagers to motor transport so that they can market their crops more effectively and obtain goods more easily which have to be purchased outside the Ukinga area.
2 *short-term* — to evaluate the demand for and viability of a commercial transport service;
   — to demonstrate the viability to village groups, entrepreneurs and financing institutions.

Plate 13 *A major road in Makete*

Plate 14 *Many roads also act as rivers*

Plate 15 *The main access to a village*

It is recognized that such a scheme will be a risky venture since, with the terrain and road conditions, operating costs will be high. Also if the scheme fails it would be more difficult for anyone else to launch a similar venture. However, the potential returns are also very high. A sack of apples (80-100 kg) retails for T.Sh.150 in Bulongwa, but (headloaded) T.Sh.750 in Mbeya. Similarly, the respective prices for a bag of wheat are said to be T.Sh.250 and 600.

It is recommended that initially the service be confined to a single vehicle such as a long-wheel-base 4-wheel-drive pick-up or a 3-tonne pay-load light truck selected from a list of 12 makes to which the Government has announced future imports will be restricted. It is proposed that the vehicle should be operated on a fully commercial basis so as to cover costs, including allowances for maintenance and depreciation. Pricing of services might also be such as to generate a surplus for future expansion of the scheme if it should prove successful.

Upgrading village roads

Most villages in Ukinga are accessible by motor vehicles although the quality of the routes serving them vary from those giving access only with extreme difficulty to a few providing for near all-year-round movement. The majority of these routes have been constructed, and are maintained, by village self-help efforts. Few all-weather roads have resulted because of:

— lack of knowledge about the techniques of earth road construction and maintenance;
— inadequate provision of culverts and bridges;
— lack of suitable crushed rock or gravel surfaces in places where indigenous soils become easily waterlogged.

Village roads in the area are low on the Government's list of priorities. In the prevailing economic climate it is considered most unlikely that funds will become available for the maintenance of Village class roads. Consequently they are only likely to be improved if present self-help efforts can be redirected and made more effective in establishing and maintaining roads which can withstand the local climatic conditions.

The most important single requirement in upgrading existing village roads is to improve their drainage since the prevailing problems centre on the waterlogging or erosion of the surface due to the uncontrolled flow of water. More specifically, it will be necessary to provide:

1. all roads with a cambered running surface and side drains;
2. lead-off drains where appropriate;
3. culverts to conduct concentrated water flows across the road;
4. spot improvements on naturally water-logging soils and very steep gradients by provision of crushed rock or gravel surfaces;
5. protection measures in side and lead-off drains;
6. selected clearing of brush and trees from the roadside to permit the surface to dry out after periods of rain;
7. for the diversion, before the side or lead-off drains are reached, of potentially erosive water flows from footpaths crossing the road formation;
8. selected widening of the road formation particularly in mountainous areas;
9. selected re-alignment to reduce gradients or the length of route; and
10. safe bridges for major streams and rivers.

To achieve these objectives it will be necessary to educate villagers in improved methods of construction and maintenance, and in some cases to supplement their efforts by technical personnel skilled in the:

1. construction and maintenance of a good road formation comprising the running surface, side and lead-off drains;
2. execution of erosion protection measures;
3. widening and re-aligning of road sections;
4. construction of culverts and bridges; and
5. excavation and crushing of rock and gravel.

The majority of these technical personnel should be recruited from and trained in the Ukinga area.

The emphasis on re-directing village self-help efforts implies that upgrading will be by labour-based rather than the normal equipment-intensive method. Such a policy is eminently suited to local conditions because:

1. of the tradition of road construction and maintenance and the availability of labour;
2. of existing acute difficulties in obtaining construction plant, fuel and spare parts;
3. the terrain — most of the roads are in hilly or mountainous side-cut — will make the operation of bulldozers and graders hazardous and extremely expensive;

4 most of the direct benefits of the investment will stay in Ukinga in the form of wages rather then be exported immediately in the form of equipment purchases;
5 it should inculcate the necessary skills to enhance the standard of future road maintenance.

Any external assistance for the upgrading of village roads should be supplementary to, rather than a replacement for, the existing voluntary system. Thus, it is not proposed to pay village labour for road work other than in exceptional circumstances. The major reason for this is the need to safeguard the future maintenance of the upgraded roads without any external assistance. Experience elsewhere suggests that if villagers were to become accustomed to being paid for work on roads it is unlikely that the tradition of voluntary maintenance will survive. However, it would be necessary to pay skilled labour during their employment on the project.

To implement village roads upgrading programmes it is proposed to set up a unit which would operate a mobile team to provide technical support to villages in improving their roads. It is proposed that the Unit should enter into a covenant with village leaders, or the leaders of a group of villages as appropriate, for the upgrading of the road linking the village(s) to a market centre of the Regional/District road system. Under the terms of the covenant the Unit would undertake to:

1 plan the improvement of the route and conduct all necessary surveys;
2 provide an estimate of material and labour requirements;
3 train selected villagers — to act as local 'gang leaders' — in basic construction skills;
4 provide any specialized tools and equipment as necessary;
5 provide overall skilled supervision;
6 undertake and provide skilled labour for the more difficult operations such as surveying and setting-out, rock crushing, haulage of material, culvert and bridge construction;
7 provide rock and timber, if unavailable from village resources, and other non-local materials, e.g. cement, wire gabions, etc.

In return the village(s) would be required to provide free of charge:

1 the labour required for an agreed duration and starting time;
2 materials such as rock and timber for bridges/culverts, if feasible, from village resources; and
3 to give a guarantee for the road's subsequent maintenance.

Summary

This chapter is the only one in the book which presents a comprehensive programme to overcome the transport problems of a specific area. In fact, the proposals made are a practical reflection of the theme of the book. That is, that any proposal to improve transport in the rural areas must take into account the actual demand, the resources available and the sustainability of the actions proposed. Whilst more roads would indeed help the people of Ukinga, it is quite clear that the economic conditions in Tanzania will allow only a marginal increase in government expenditure for road construction. It is therefore important to look for alternatives which can complement the limited road network available. In the case of roadworks a scheme similar to the one proposed for the Ukinga area was operating very successfully in Afghanistan[4], illustrating that alternative approaches of this nature are certainly a feasible proposition.

Since the time of the study, both the Government and the donor community have shown great interest in this project. It is hoped that it will be implemented in the near future.

CHAPTER 9

Bangladesh Rural Transport Study[†]

Introduction

Rural transport facilities in Bangladesh are extremely poorly developed. The Planning Commission has estimated that 80 per cent of the 68,000 villages have no direct access to mechanized transport facilities.[1] For the major part of their travel the rural population rely on non-motorized means such as rickshaws, bullock carts, country boats, and bicycles. This study was initiated by the Government to investigate the present and likely future needs for rural transport. The distinctive feature of the study was its focus on the role and consequences of rural transport improvements in relation to rural development. In particular, the study was one of the few to have raised doubts about the causal relationship between transport and development.

A sample of five *thanas* (administrative units) was used, although certain biases relating to farm size and accessibility were included. In selecting the *thanas*, an attempt was made to take account of seasonal and geographical variations. The study was carried out between 1975 and 1977.

Background

The inspiration for this study came from two sources. The first of these was the Bangladesh Transport Survey completed in 1974. This concentrated on the main inter-district arterial transport system and its results incorporated numerous assumptions about the movement of goods in rural areas. There remained a need to investigate the transport of agricultural commodities from farm gate to primary and secondary markets: these movements occur

---

[†]This chapter is based on the study carried out by the Planning Commission of the Government of Bangladesh with advisory services from the Overseas Development Group of the University of East Anglia, United Kingdom.

before the arterial system is reached. Secondly, considerable rural development work has been carried out in Bangladesh since the early 1960s involving the introduction of irrigation, fertilizers and high-yield varieties of seeds, and resulting in a considerable increase in agricultural production. Consequently, there has been an increased demand for transport of both agricultural inputs, in the form of fertilizers and diesel oil for irrigation pumps, and of outputs as a result of a considerably increased volume of marketable surplus. In most development proposals and feasibility studies, it has been assumed that the existing rural transport systems can cope with this increased demand although little detailed information about these present systems is available. In particular, it is not known whether they are a real limitation to development efforts.

The study was devised to find out the present methods of rural transport, their costs, capacity to absorb the increased traffic consequent upon development programmes, variations within the country and between seasons in rural transport methods, and how the agricultural commodities get from the farm gate to the arterial transport system. The study also examined the movement of goods between farmers and traders and the extent to which rural transport is a constraint upon rural development. Two specific objectives of the study were to establish:

1 present and likely future methods of rural transport and how they might feed into the arterial network;
2 an appropriate methodology by which rural transport considerations can be included within overall rural development planning.

Study approach

Bangladesh exhibits considerable geographical and seasonal variations and the collection of information on rural production, consumption and transport to illustrate this variety would be nearly impossible. The approach used was to select five *thanas* (administrative units), from the 415 that comprise Bangladesh, as study areas (see Figure 10). The study areas chosen were selected to take account of the seasonal and geographic differences in Bangladesh and the different levels of rural development that are already found. In addition to normal base data collection, observations and interviews were conducted at a sample of the different 'levels' of rural markets; interviews were also conducted with a further sample of farmers.

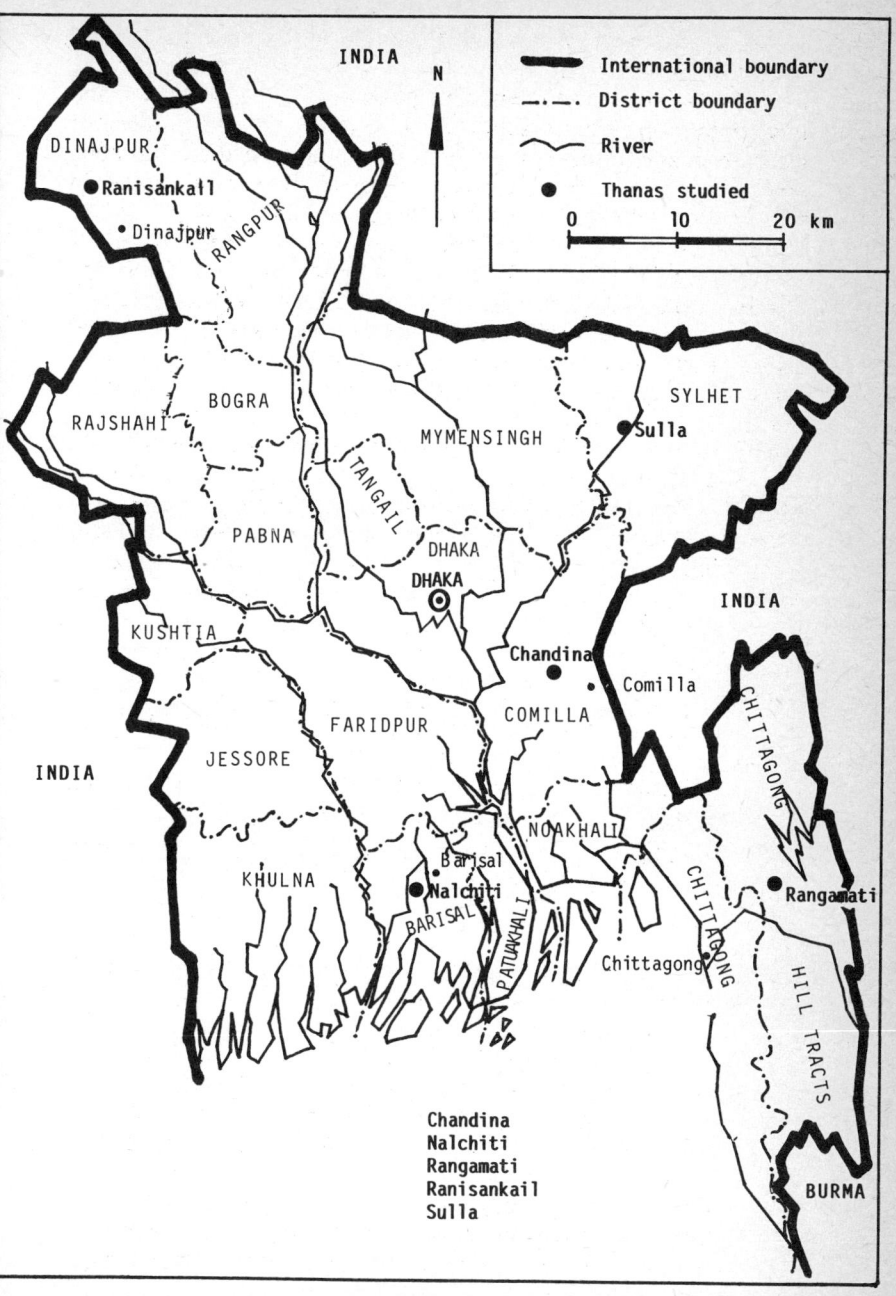

Fig. 10 *Location of Thanas studied*

The study methodology gave rise to two biases in the results. First, the size of the survey team itself led to transport and accommodation problems and this meant that only in exceptional circumstances was it possible to include areas of the country at considerable distances from main roads.[2] Second, the method of selecting farmers for interview also biased the results. The bias derived from the assumption that the surplus food in any area of Bangladesh is produced and marketed by the large farmers, and thus it is they that have the greatest call on the transport facilities in an area. It was, as a consequence of this assumption, thought important to ensure that a representative sample of these large farmers were selected. In the light of the material collected in the study it now appears that the small farmers, because they sell and buy paddy and rice, are also heavy utilizers of the transport facilities. Their vastly superior numbers means that a more representative sampling method would have been desirable. The deliberately biased sample taken of large farmers was made less representative by the method which had to be chosen to select the farmers to be interviewed in each size group. Because of the shortage of time it was not possible for the investigators to visit each farmer in his home. This would have involved long journeys, on foot in many cases. Rather the local Union[3] Council officers were notified in advance of the survey, its purpose and the desired nature of the sample of farmers. The farmers thus selected were asked to be available at the union headquarters on the appropriate day. This undoubtedly biased the sample towards the 'developed' farms and the larger ones in each size group. In the last *thana* to be studied the sampling frame was changed and in each union of the *thana* two villages were selected, one close to a main road and one more distant from good transport, and a 10 per cent sample of all farms within these villages was studied.

Findings of the study

The main points to emerge from the study can be summarized as follows:

1 The small farmers have a need for frequent marketing of small quantities of goods. This is reflected in the purchase of about as much rice or paddy as is sold and in the generally small loads carried to market by farmers over very short distances. These sales immediately after harvest are necessary partly to repay debts (see 6 below) and partly because of a lack of suitable storage (see 2 below).

2 A lack of suitable storage on farms and of credit for farmers are the main reasons why paddy has to be sold shortly after harvest rather than kept for use later in the year. In one of the study areas between 30 and 40 per cent of the paddy is sold within two weeks of harvest either to repay debts or because of lack of storage. Prices are lowest after harvest because of the resulting glut. Small farmers are particularly short of storage. Improving storage, perhaps on a village rather than a farm level, would reduce the necessity to buy and sell the same products at different times of the year. In one area, for example, the small farmers sell 17 per cent of their harvested paddy (mostly directly after the harvest) and they re-buy the equivalent of 26 per cent later in the year. Improved storage would also spread the sale of paddy over a longer period of time. Both these developments would reduce the strain on rural transport facilities available for producers who have a genuine surplus.
3 Dissatisfaction expressed with the state of transport in rural areas is, at least in part, a result of a lack of vehicles, especially country boats[14], which therefore ties the small farmer to the local market where he is in the hands of a very limited number of traders and receives a low price for his paddy (see 7 below and Table 41).
4 Fertilizer distribution benefits the large farmers. This is partly because access to the fertilizer supplies through the important markets is easier for the large farmer who has his own transport, and partly because the large farmer is financially in a better position to make the unofficial payments necessary to obtain these resources.
5 Access to irrigation pumps and irrigation water is similarly limited to the large farmers.
6 The role of traders in the marketing of rice and other products and in the provision of credit to farmers is of the greatest importance. Most farmers are in the hands of a very small number of traders when selling in the local markets. These traders advance money to buy inputs and food before harvest in return for a share of the paddy at harvest time. This share is 'bought' at a price that ensures a very high interest rate to the trader. Without this credit many farmers would be forced to sell their land or, if they are sharecroppers, to move to cities where ration supplies are more readily available, or to find work as labourers on farms or food-for-work programmes. Access to government credit is time-consuming and difficult. Credit agencies are often at a considerable distance and mak-

ing these journeys may absorb up to 25 per cent of the credit applied for.
7. Rice procurement favours the large farmers and traders. Access to the limited number of procurement centres is relatively easy for these groups and, because of their larger volume of rice for sale, also relatively cheaper. As long as rice marketing is tied to the provision of credit, the government rice procurement programme will have limited effects on the small farmers who are obliged to sell to the traders who provide the credit.
8. Production, storage, marketing and credit form a closely connected quartet and development work and investment should not consider one without an assessment of its impact on the other three.
9. Rural transport is difficult over much of Bangladesh but it does not at present provide the only constraint to agricultural development. The vast majority of Bangladeshi farmers cultivate very small acreages and the constraints limiting their increased production are associated with unequal access to resources (particularly credit and agriculture inputs) and tied marketing arrangements with traders where competition is limited. To improve rural transport alone in this situation is likely to provide greater advantages to the larger farmers and to the traders, both groups having their own transport (bullock carts and country boats). Transport development should be conceived as part of an overall rural development package aimed at improving conditions for small and large farmers.
10. Present rural transport is slow and labour-intensive but there are few commodities for which speed is essential, and rural labour supply is abundant and growing. Most transport infrastructure improvements, while providing employment during their construction, reduce the total labour requirements in the transport sector in the long run. Agricultural improvements of all sorts have in the past encouraged a concentration of land holding in fewer hands and an increase in the number of share-croppers and landless labourers. *Improvement of transport facilities alone is likely to accelerate this trend by providing further advantage to bigger farmers*. Transport demand is at present highly seasonal and the peak demands could be reduced and levelled out by improvements in credit and rural storage. Some paddy is sold at the same time as the sale of small amounts of perishable goods such as vegetables and eggs. However, if the need to sell crops, especially paddy, directly after harvest can be reduced through local storage

Table 41. Country Boat Ownership (%) in Relation to Size of Holding (ha)[1]

Survey area	Operational holding (ha)		
	0-1.6	1.6-4.0	+4.0
1	Little used except in some areas in the wet season only		
2	36	N/A	76
3	18	46	60
4	Little used anywhere in survey area		
5	55	75	95

[1] Ownership is not only a function of size of holding (wealth) but also of location. Bangladesh is subject to seasonal flooding. In some cases this is extreme and all land transport ceases for several months: boat ownership is virtually essential to survival; in other areas — for example, the north-west — little, if any, flooding occurs and land transport dominates. Many coastal and some inland areas of Bangladesh are only accessible by water.

and credit availability, the capacity of the existing rural transport facilities should, with some improvements, be adequate to cope with increased agricultural output. Small farmers rarely employ labour, relying on that of their families, and any reduction in marketing time would be a net gain to the productive employment of that family.

11 In areas where the cropping ratio is high and the scope for further increase in productivity is limited, the main need for improved speed of travel is for the movement of skilled and experienced manpower. Because, under existing arrangements, this is in short supply for health care, family planning, agricultural extension services, etc., the few people who are available have to be mobile and have quick access to rural areas. They cannot be based in dispersed locations without a substantial increase in their numbers. Thus, the movement of manpower into rural areas, rather than an improvement in the movement of goods out, may provide a justification for rural road construction and other transport improvements. In this case, the detailed priorities for road construction and improvement become fairly obvious: first, access to the *thana* headquarters or major population centre and from there, access into the interior of the *thana*, probably by means of a spine road or routeway more or less down the centre.

The study findings suggested that the transport of goods and freight does present a problem in the rural areas of Bangladesh. Nevertheless, they also reveal that the conventional response to this problem — the provision of transport infrastructure — may not be appropriate. In the first place, lack of transport is only one of a large range of obstacles that impeded development. Providing it will not, automatically, lead to development. Moreover, other solutions to the problems posed by lack of transport may be more cost-effective and may benefit a larger number of the population. The reallocation of services, the provision of storage for paddy, better credit facilities, access to simple vehicles would all help to solve problems which are presently seen to be the fault of transport. Unlike most of its predecessors, and many of its successors, this study did not assume that the solution to the lack of transport was necessarily the provision of roads. Indeed it suggested that there could be other, more cost-effective, ways of solving the problem. This naturally led to a reassessment of appraisal methodology.

In Bangladesh, as in many parts of the world, the assessment of the benefits of transport improvements has been based on the estimation of the savings to existing users of the transport facility and an allowance for the benefits generated by the investment. As far as user savings were concerned the levels of traffic were such that the benefits so derived were unlikely to justify anything but the most meagre investment. The study indicated that the most likely generated traffic benefits would result from an increase in agricultural production.

The evidence suggested that such effects were likely to be small. For most crops, transport costs represent only a small proportion of the market price. Therefore, reductions in transport costs alone would offer little incentive to increase production. Similarly, transport costs represent only a small part of the cost of farm inputs such as fertilizer (approximately 5 per cent for urea) and therefore transport cost reductions are unlikely to lead to significant increases in use of these inputs. Probably one of the few situations where transport improvements would have a dramatic effect on production would be where new land can be brought into cultivation or where the cropping ratio can be substantially improved. Such situations are rare in most parts of Bangladesh. Generally speaking, the benefits to generated traffic are likely to be fairly low and unlikely to significantly alter the conclusions reached on the basis of normal traffic unless other obstacles to increased output can be overcome.

The general conclusion therefore was that, whilst transport was one of the constraints to development, large investments in transport *alone* could not be justified because:

— other constraints would still effectively limit development;
— road improvements would merely benefit the minority élite who were able to take advantage of the investment.

Summary

The study findings argued strongly for the assessment of alternative ways to solve the transport problem. In subsequent work, the Planning Commission has described one element which merits serious consideration — the local transport system. The study noted that one of the serious constraints was the lack of access to even the most simple vehicles. If attention were focused on this, the local transport system might be able to play its proper role as a complement to the national system. In Bangladesh, 50 per cent of the population are more than 10 km from the recognized transport network. Non-motorized transport, and in particular head and shoulder loading, dominates rural transport. In the riverine parts of the country, simple boats driven by oars and muscle power are the only means of transport. The Planning Commission has estimated that non-motorized transport accounts for more than half of freight and passenger movements in rural Bangladesh. As far as transport is concerned therefore, it would appear that investments in improving the quality of non-motorized vehicles would be equally profitable as investments in road improvements.

The work carried out by the Planning Commission and its advisers is of particular interest because it eschews the conventional formula that investments in rural transport will result in rural development. It accepts that transport is one of the constraints to development but must be viewed in conjunction with the other identified constraints. Equally transport is understood to have two distinct and complementary elements: the national system, upon which previous attention has been focused, and the local transport system, which has been generally ignored.

CHAPTER 10

Transport for Small Farmers in Kenya

Introduction

For the final case study we return to Kenya. Charles Kaira's study, described in Chapter 4, was concerned with a detailed comparison of transport patterns in two villages. This study is concerned more with general transport policy and how it affects small farmers.

In Kenya, there are over 1.5 million small farms, most of which are less than 5 ha. The study was carried out by John Howe as part of a general evaluation of how transport planning in Kenya affected these farmers. Whilst it is somewhat dated, having been carried out in 1976, it does provide a sound description of how transport constrains the development of small-farmer agriculture.

Background

The study is based on a short-term field investigation carried out in 1976. The investigation drew upon published statistics, data drawn from other studies and surveys, and information obtained from informal interviews with farmers, transporters, local government officials and other key informants.

Study findings

All small farmers in Kenya need transport for the production and marketing of crops and livestock, and household activities. However, the survey revealed a wide variety in the specific transport requirements of different farmers, depending on the crops grown, number of livestock owned, size of farms, distance to market outlets, and the range of inputs used. This variety is reflected in Table 42, which summarizes the findings regarding frequency of trips, trip purposes, typical loads, distances and pathway conditions associated with the different transport requirements. The figures suggest that most important needs can be characterized as the movement of small loads (10-150 kg units) over relatively short distances (1-25 km). On-farm the range of loads is likely to be the same, but the typical distances are shorter (1-13 km).

Table 42. Transport Requirements of Small Farmers

Group involved	Trip purpose	Frequency	Load	Distance	Conditions
All small farmers	On-farm transport connected with subsistence: transport of food products from plot to dwelling	Daily	Very small 10 kg	Very short 1 km	Off-road
All small farmers above subsistence level	On-farm transport connected with commercial farming: transport of products and inputs from fields to storage area	Follows agricultural schedule: varies with crops	Depends on yields, increases with acreage under cultivation or grazing	Increases with acreage: 1-2 km	Off-road
All small farmers	Gathering of water and fuel from areas near farm	Probably daily	50 kg water and 30 kg firewood	Depends on available supplies: 2-13 km quoted	Primarily off-road
All small farmers above subsistence level	Trips to local market: transport of surplus products from farm to market and purchased products back from market to farm	Daily, twice a week or weekly; depending on market schedule	Depends on yield, acreage, transport capacity: 15-150 kg	Up to 25 km: average 5-15 km	Part off-road, part on-road
All small farmers producing cotton, coffee, tea or pyrethrum	Transport of cash crops to collection points, depots or buying centres	Depends on harvesting schedule, perishability of product	Depends on yields, acreage, transport capacity	5-10 km average	Part off-road, part on-road
All small farmers producing milk, maize and food crops not sold at farmgate	Transport of surplus food products to collection points, depots, or cooling centres	Depends on harvesting schedule, perishability of product; daily for milk	Depends on yield, acreage, transport capacity	5-25 km average	Part off-road, part on-road
All small farmers using purchased inputs such as fertilizers, chemicals, special seeds	Transport of inputs from buying centre or stores	Follows agricultural schedule; varies with crops	Increases with acreage; minimum 50 kg bag	5-25 km average	Part off-road, part on-road
Most small farmers	Trips to major towns for special goods or services	Probably once a month on average	Usually small: 30 kg	Up to 50 km	Primarily on-road

On-farm transport

On-farm transport is required for a variety of tasks related to crop production and household needs. Movement of seeds, fodder, fertilizer and other inputs, as well as movement of harvested crops, is required each season as part of normal farming operations. Also, firewood and water must be gathered from areas surrounding the farm for the household. Since the farmer must follow a fairly rigid schedule to obtain desired yields, it is important that on-farm transport should not be so time-consuming as to delay important operations.

The degree to which on-farm transport becomes a bottleneck depends on the pool of labour available, the size of the fields and their position relative to dwellings and storage areas, and the abundance of supplies of water and fuel. Although traditional methods such as headloading and, in some areas, animals have been adequate in the past for on-farm movements, the introduction of new inputs and high-yielding seed varieties is beginning to strain the available transport capacity. While loads and distances are manageable for some tasks, such as milking cows or gathering food for meals, other on-farm transport tasks are very time-consuming, particularly the gathering of fuel and water. It has been estimated that women and children in the rural areas spend an average of three to six hours per day gathering water for home use. In cases where additional water is required for crop spraying or livestock, on-farm transport is even more burdensome and can contribute to lowered yields by interfering with the timeliness of farm operations, if headloading is the only form of movement.[1]

Transport of inputs to the farm

An important requirement of the farmer, related to crop production, is the transport of inputs from market outlets to the farm. The most important purchased inputs used on small farms in Kenya include fertilizer, insecticides for crops in storage and in the field, and seeds. Use of these purchased inputs has always been high in the large farm areas, but only recently have they been promoted among smallholders, and the distribution network is relatively thin and underdeveloped.

Of the two main distribution channels for inputs, the Kenya Farmers Association Limited (KFA) has the most comprehensive coverage. In the early 1970s, over half of total KFA sales went to smaller farmers. However, because of fixed margins for stockists, which do not include transport costs, smaller and less commercialized farmers in remote areas were effectively excluded from access to inputs sold by KFA agents. In response to the need of some of these farmers, the co-operative movement began to play a role in input distribution through a new merchandising branch of the Kenya National Federation of Co-operatives (KNFC). Distances to KFA and co-operative stores generally range from 5-25 km on average, but there is considerable variation depending on the effectiveness of the distribution network in the area. The loads involved vary with the acreage of crops under cultivation. For some inputs such as fertilizer, however, a 50 kg bag is the minimum quantity available, and this is too heavy to be carried any distance by headloading. The problems small famers experience in obtaining inputs are therefore due in part to lack of appropriate transport alternatives as well as the limited network of KFA and KNFC distributors. These transport and distribution problems have had serious consequences in some areas; the failure to obtain needed inputs at the correct time has been an important factor holding down yields among smallholders.

Transport of outputs for marketing
Another important requirement for the smallholder is the transport of agricultural products to market for sale. The market outlets available to the small farmer in Kenya include local market places, itinerant traders, co-operative marketing societies, and official agents of statutory authorities such as the Maize and Produce Board.

As yields increase on existing farms, as new lands are opened up for cultivation, and as improved inputs are accepted by small farmers, transport requirements increase. A typical smallholder participating in the Integrated Agricultural Development Project is expected over a four-year period to increase his annual output from 5.5 tonnes to 12.6 tonnes. Most of the increase in production will be for sale and will require transport to a market outlet.

For major export and cash crops such as coffee, tea, passion fruit and pyrethrum, collection services are well organized by co-operatives and traders, and collection points in many areas are within a reasonable distance of the farmer. In tea growing areas, for example, roads constructed specifically to serve the tea industry allow efficient collection services which require farmers to travel no more than 5 km to collection points.

For farmers growing foodcrops however, few market outlets are available. Although the Maize and Produce Board has a number of agents who purchase produce on their behalf, there are too few of these agents to provide a marketing outlet within easy reach of most farmers. Co-operative collection services for minor food crops such as pulses, potatoes, peas, sorghum and millet are virtually non-existent. Although there are over 200 multi-produce co-operative societies in Kenya which handle these food crops, many do not consider the provision of collection services to be one of their functions. Among those co-operatives who provide limited collection services, there seems to be a general lack of transport capacity and a shortage of buying centres.

For many small farmers growing foodcrops, then, the only market outlets available are the local market places and the private traders. Most local market places operate on a regular schedule and are within 5-15 km of small farmers. In areas where agricultural potential or population density is low, the farmer may have to travel longer distances to get to the market place. Although the aggregate amount traded in these market places is quite large, individual trading generally involves small amounts.

Farmers who produce a large surplus of food crops often sell to itinerant traders as well as in the market place. Since the traders operate pick-ups which can penetrate many areas, these farmers only have to transport their goods a short distance to the roadside. However, there are reports that prices offered by the traders are extremely low and many smallholders would like to seek other market outlets, but have no alternative transport. Farmers growing low-value, bulky, perishable foodcrops such as potatoes are particularly dependent on itinerant traders since they lack the transport capacity to carry large, heavy loads to the local market place for sale.

In the Meru and Embu regions, for example, problems with transport limited the cultivation of areas which had a high agricultural potential. The higher zones of the Meru region are among the most important potato producing areas of the country. Yields are very high (18-22.5 tonnes per ha) and a relatively small plot can be an excellent source of cash earnings. However, most of the potatoes are harvested over a relatively short period and, with no storage facilities, large quantities must be transported promptly to the market to avoid spoilage. Indeed, it is a matter of record that in most normal years the farmers have been dependent on traders who circulate among them offering low prices related more often to the farmers' transport difficulties than to actual values. For example, in one area it was reported that farmers were selling potatoes at the farmgate for K.Sh.25-40 per bag as against a selling price of as much as K.Sh.150-200 per bag, in the capital. As typical round-trip transportation costs from the area to the capital are no more than K.Sh.8-10 per bag, the income to the trader from sale of the produce is substantially higher than that to the farmer. However, it does relieve the farmer of the need to negotiate supply and delivery of the produce to buyers in the capital.

Limited milk production by smallholders is a common example of agricultural yields held back by transport constraints. Although the services collecting and transporting milk to the creameries appear to be efficient, movement of milk from the farms to collection points has proven to be a time-consuming activity which limits production in some regions (Nakuru, Kericho, Meru and Embu). Because there is a lack of cooling facilities on small farms, the milk must be transported daily by bicycle or by hand to the nearest collection point. Throughout Kenya, this lack of transportation and storage produces a pattern of selling only the morning milk, while the evening production is consumed at home, fed to calves, sold among any interested neighbours, or simply wasted. Officials estimate that in some areas as much as 10-30 per cent of the milk yield may be wasted. A serious constraint to increased production results since the farmer realizes that increasing overall yields will also raise the amount of evening milk for which he has no cash market. In certain areas the Agricultural Finance Corporation has established a maximum loan limit for dairy cows until the problem of collecting evening milk is resolved.

Transport modes used by Kenyan smallholders
A variety of transport methods are used by small farmers to meet their requirements. Headloading is by far the most common method, being used for on-farm transport, gathering of fuel and water, and trips to and from marketing outlets. Surveys some years ago showed that over 90 per cent of rural trips were on foot, 4 per cent by bicycle and just 2.5 per cent by motorized transport.[2,3] Wheelbarrows and animal-drawn carts or sledges are also used by some farmers for on-farm transport and gathering of water and fuel supplies, but only in a few areas are they common.

Transport by tractor and trailer is relatively rare in small farm areas. Tractor hire services provided by entrepreneurs and the Government are generally confined to ploughing, which is more profitable. The tractors available are mostly 50-60 hp units which have relatively limited transport capability despite their high power output.

Motorized road vehicles are available to small farmers in the form of buses, *matatus*, and small pick-up trucks available for hire. While buses and *matatus* are used widely by small farmers for longer trips, the pick-up trucks for hire provide services only indirectly through private traders and co-operative collection services. These entrepreneurial services are filling many of the important transport needs of smallholders, but only for those located close to the main roads.

Costs and charges for transport
Table 43 gives a summary of estimated costs and charges of the different forms of transport used by farmers. Many of these figures must be treated with caution since the evidence upon which they are based is fragmentary. It is clear that for buses and *matatus* the unit cost is dependent upon the distance travelled: the shorter the distance, the higher the unit cost. Although some of the figures are imprecise, the main conclusions are fairly robust.

1. For short-distance trips, which are the norm for most smallholders, charges can exceed costs by a factor of 10 or more if bus, taxi, or ox-cart are used.
2. For short-distance trips, the cost of most primitive forms of transport — donkeys and headloading — is relatively very expensive. This is partly because of their slowness. However, costs of these modes are critically dependent upon the value assumed for operator time. A value of K.Sh.3 per day was used, which was the lowest quoted wage rate for rural labour.
3. For journeys from the roadside to market, *matatu* transport is probably the most expensive to the smallholder. It also appeared to be one of the most common.

Table 43. Summary of Rural Goods Transport Costs and Charges[1] (July 1976 prices)

Means of goods movement	Cost K.Sh./tonne km	Charge K.Sh./tonne km
Lorry	0.3	2
Bus	0.4-0.7	1-80
Matatu	0.5-0.6	1-100
Tractor and trailer	1.6.-6.0	2-13
Ox-cart (2 oxen)	0.8	2.3-13.9
Donkey	5.6	18-42
Bicycle	1.6	NA[2]
Headloading	17	31-63

[1] A range of values is given for costs because of uncertainty in the data and doubts about average load factors, availability of return loads etc. The range of values for charges is because rates are dictated by bargaining and what the market will bear. Usually charges are per bag, giving very high rates for short distances.

[2] Not operated for hire.

4 Ox-carts offer the potentially lowest cost of transport to the smallholder for on-farm and farm-to-roadside goods movement, although this is dependent upon the load factor assumed.

In considering these conclusions it is vital to bear in mind that of equal, if not more, importance to transport costs and charges are:

— the choice available to the farmer; and
— what he can afford to buy for himself where conventional services are not available.

If there is no sensible alternative, the fact that a particular mode of transport is costly is largely immaterial. In the study area, lorry services were uncommon because of the generally scattered and small consignments offered by smallholders. Buses were largely confined to the main roads and few tractors and ox-carts were engaged in transport for hire. This probably accounts for the high charges *matatus* were able to command: in many cases they were the only service available.

If conventional transport services are scarce or expensive, and the marketing and co-operative organizations are unable to organize collection and delivery for the smallholder, he must fend for himself. The critical factor in improving the transport available to the smallholder then becomes affordability. The very low unit costs of movement that lorries and pick-ups can achieve are immaterial to the farmer who cannot afford such vehicles. An ILO survey in 1972 showed that most smallholders' net incomes from farming were limited to K.Sh.4,000 or less.[4,5]

In general, expenditure on transport averaged 3 per cent of total expenditure and for the majority of small farmers this would amount to less than K.Sh.100/annum). These figures indicate that the purchase of the cheapest conventional motorized vehicle (pickup, K.Sh.40,000) was beyond practical consideration. Even oxen (K.Sh.420-600 each), an ox-cart (K.Sh.1,000-1,500), a bicycle (K.Sh.850) or a wheelbarrow (K.Sh.300) would have represented a significant investment. At present levels of development simple vehicles may be the only means of transport the majority of smallholders can afford to own.

Summary

The survey indicated that transport is indeed a major problem for small farmers. Not, however, in the sense that would be immediately detectable by standard methods of economic appraisal. For, in fact, transport charges account for a very minor part of the selling price of crops. It is in its effect as an inhibitor that the lack of suitable transport is evident as a constraint to development of smallholder agriculture.

The forms of transport available to the small farmer are simple and low cost. They are also capable of carrying small loads over short distances. Policies in relation to agricultural production however tend to be in conflict with this type of transport. New varieties of seed and the attendant fertilizers imply increased transport demands. In general, the distribution system does not reach the small farmer and the inputs are packaged in such a way that they are too big to be transported by the means at his disposal. As far as outputs are concerned, the transport facilities for major export crops are available. However those for minor food crops such as potatoes, sorghum and millet are virtually non-existent. Many small farmers are therefore dependent on traders who can dictate the price.

PART IV — SUMMARY

CHAPTER 11

Conclusions and Policy Implications

The case studies have illustrated the argument set out in the Introduction that a local transport system exists; that in many communities it is thriving; that economic and social development could not take place without it; and, paradoxically, that it has been generally ignored by planners. This local transport system is complementary to the national one and takes over where the other leaves off. It seems clear that the local system merits a great deal more attention than it has been given hitherto. These studies are a first step in that direction.

Given the variety of climatic, social and political conditions encompassed by the studies, it is perhaps rather surprising that there is a considerable degree of commonality in their findings and that there are general conclusions to be drawn from them. In the following sections, we have attempted to identify the major findings and, in so doing, lay the basis for a reorientation in the approach to rural transport planning.

1   Access to the transport system

The fact that the majority of the rural population of developing countries do not have direct access to a recognizable road is a clear enough indication that transport planning has not been explicitly concerned with people and their transport needs. In the Philippines, for example, less than half the rural villages were said to have access to the road system. In Bangladesh the situation is worse with 80 per cent of the villages having no direct access to mechanized means of transport. Evidence from other sources shows that in India (1978) about 70 per cent of villages did not have all-weather road connections, and 55 per cent of villages were not connected to any type of road.[1] Also, in a comparatively wealthy country such as Egypt, 32 per cent of villages were connected to larger villages, and thence the road network, only by footpaths.[2] Although not quantified, lack of road access was clearly a significant aspect of the studies in Nigeria, the Republic of Korea, Tanzania and Western Samoa. Moreover, it was clear from most of the studies that the majority of rural communities would, for the foreseeable future, be dependent upon footpaths and tracks, rather than engineered roads, for the bulk of their movement needs despite the best efforts of the respective governments to extend the road network.

The correlation between quality of route and the existence and reliability of public transport services (observed previously in the Philippines, Sierra Leone, Tunisia and India[3]) was confirmed by the study in Tanzania: for six months of the year (the rainy season) services simply cease. The evidence also suggests that the poor make only infrequent use of public transport services. In the Philippines, for example, the people using hire-and-reward passenger services have incomes at or about the median income level.[4]

The situation described above has not arisen, one should hasten to add, because of the callousness or insensitivity of planners. It is a natural result of an exaggerated concern with economic rather than socio-economic development. Thus, in Kenya, roads related to the exploitation of export crops are well established. On the other hand, roads serving small farmers working to sell surplus food crops were less well developed. In Tanzania, the perceived demand was for roads to exploit pyrethrum; the actual demand, as established by the study, included a real desire for better access to health facilities.

As many of the case studies show, the local transport system used by the majority of rural people is, of necessity, complementary to the 'national' transport system. It has not developed because of any rational planning. What is evident is that this part of the transport system is not well understood by government planners and their international advisers, whose perception of rural transport is exemplified by lorries laden with crops for sale and vehicles taking busy officials about their business. For the rural inhabitants, on the other hand, the local transport system is the means to simplify the attainment of basic needs such as food, clothing, shelter, education and health.

2 The characteristics of local level transport

The studies provide valuable information on the nature of local level transport in terms of travel demand patterns, vehicle ownership, modal distribution and frequency.

The studies show that it is important to differentiate between on-farm and off-farm transport. The former comprises movements related to domestic needs, such as water and firewood gathering, smallholder cultivation, grazing of animals and transport of farm inputs and outputs. On-farm transport generally takes place away from a recognized road. Off-farm transport comprises trips to the market, to visit friends or to reach certain social amenities, for example, schools and health clinics. Off-farm transport relates more to the conventional perception of transport in that at least some of it takes place on a recognizable road and, sometimes, with a motorized vehicle.

2.1 The purpose of local level transport

Evaluation of rural transport is conventionally focused on off-farm transport and, in particular, on the increase in agricultural production that is produced by the construction or improvement of a road. The evaluation therefore assumes that rural transport demand is mainly related to agricultural production and that trips for agricultural purposes are predominant.

The studies reveal a somewhat different picture. In the first place, people in the rural areas are more mobile than has previously been assumed. The evidence from the studies suggests that each member of a rural household will make at least one and sometimes two recognizable journeys each day. Secondly, the studies show that trips related to the marketing of agricultural production are in the minority; an important minority indeed, but other trips make up the majority of rural transport.

Kaira's detailed analysis of local level transport in Kenya, for example, shows that only a minority of trips were related to shopping or marketing. Trips for leisure, for farming activities and for household tasks, such as water and wood collection, were of equal if not greater importance. In Nigeria, trips to the market represented less than 10 per cent of the total.

The Kenya study indicated that, apart from transport of farm products during harvest, it is water collection that poses the primary daily movement problem to the subsistence household. The majority of trips involving the carriage of a load are for water and wood collection. A recent study in Southern and East Africa confirmed that in an average family of six or seven, one person's sole job is to collect firewood.[5]

Long distance trips in Kenya were described as being 'compulsory' visits to facilities unavailable in the village, such as hospitals and shops. A World Bank study in Mexico[6] found that out-of-village trips were approximately evenly divided between work-related travel and general purpose (shopping/business/social) visits, though in the more remote areas work-related travel predominated. A village level study in Tanzania[7] described travel for non-economic (social or medical) purposes as being 'relatively important' with familial ties providing the major reason for social trips.

2.2 Length and loads transported

Table 44 summarizes the data available from the studies. In general, the conclusion of the Kenyan study can be applied to all the studies. That is, the transport needs of the rural population can be characterized as the movement of small loads over relatively short distances.

Trips of less than 7 km comprise the majority in Kenya, Malaysia, India and Western Samoa. As one would expect, on-farm trips are generally short. However even in India, where 'on-farm' was understood as being within the community, the average trip distance was 1.5 km. Off-farm trips were generally longer but few were over 12 km long.

The evidence regarding the average size of loads is more limited but suggests that most trips are concerned with relatively small loads of between 25 and 50 kg. Other, indirect evidence from the studies seems to support this. Thus, even where crops are being transported, each household has relatively little to transport — 500 kg of each crop per year in Kenya. Again in Kenya, water and wood collection comprised a considerable proportion of the journeys made. These would generally amount to loads of 30-50 kg per trip.

2.3 Modes of local transport

The predominant means of transport in the rural areas of developing countries is on foot. Even in a country as relatively prosperous as Malaysia 70 per cent of all on-farm trips, 60 per cent of all school trips and 50 per cent of shopping trips were on foot. In Kenya, over 70 per cent of all trips were on foot. The same level can be deduced in India, where over 70 per cent of households do not own any form of transport.

Walking remains the major means of movement for short journeys, and for some longer ones, with loads carried on the head (Kenya, Tanzania), the back (Republic of Korea) and the shoulder (Malaysia). It is noteworthy how even very simple load-carrying devices, such as the *chee-geh*, have subtle design features adapted to local conditions. There are also, for example, a variety of versions of the shoulder pole, referred to in the Malaysian study, for different applications. The dimensions and material of the pole are usually such that it is flexible and moves in time with

Table 44. Length and Loads of Rural Transport

	Kenya	Malaysia	India	Bangladesh	Western Samoa	Republic of Korea
Typical distance of transport	90% of trips <7 km	75% of trips <7 km	90% of trips <5 km	Most trips <12 km	Most trips <5 km	Most trips 10 km
Average on-farm distance	0.8 km	1 km	1.5 km			
Average off-farm distance		10 km	8.3 km			
Loads transported	70% of trips <25 kg			Most trips <50 kg	Most trips <80 kg	30-80 kg

the carrier's walking rhythm, thus cushioning his shoulder from the load. There is limited evidence (Tanzania) of the use of wheelbarrows for load carrying. In China[8], wheelbarrows of a different configuration from that found elsewhere are used extensively for the movement of goods in rural areas.

The studies illustrate the widespread popularity of the bicycle throughout the developing world as a means of personal transport, and a load carrier. A variety of locally made attachments are fitted to bicycles to facilitate the carrying of different loads. The studies make limited mention, through the references to tricycles in Malaysia and pedal rickshaws in Bangladesh, of adaptations of the bicycle to increase its load carrying capacity. In China and Indonesia, the back wheels of the bicycle are strengthened to increase the load carrying capacity. In some French-speaking countries, two-wheeled trailers are commonly towed behind bicycles. This reflects practice in some parts of Europe, including Switzerland, where bicycle trailers are one of the methods used by the Post Office to deliver letters and parcels.

The studies illustrate the range of ways in which work animals can be used for transport — as pack animals (donkeys in Nigeria), to pull sledges (buffaloes in the Philippines) and to haul carts (bullocks in India). The use of animals for transport obviously complements agricultural practices based on the use of animal power. It is also worth noting that the consideration of animals for transport has generally developed as a by-product of the renewed interest in the use of animals in agriculture.

The Philippine study describes a low-cost motorized means of transport, the motor cycle and sidecar. In Malaysia, motorcycles are used to carry agricultural produce and the study proposes the use of trailers to increase their capacity. In Asian countries where two-wheeled (single axle) tractors have been adopted in agriculture, they are also widely used, with a trailer attached, for transport. In parts of Greece simple, low-cost three-wheeled diesel-engined vehicles have become popular amongst small-scale farmers.

The studies reflect the diversity of transport modes that exist in the developing world. Moreover, they indicate the extent of the use of low-cost forms of transport. This is the case in countries such as India, with low per capita incomes and very low motor vehicle ownership levels; in China which has adopted an official policy of emphasizing the use of non-motorized modes to meet local level rural transport needs; and even in petroleum producing and exporting countries such as Indonesia.[9] The popularity of these forms of transport results from the fact that they suit local requirements and because, being low-cost, they are affordable. It is obvious that the purchase of a car or pick-up is quite beyond the means of most rural people in most developing countries. Low-cost vehicles are more widely affordable, and hence available. Personal ownership of a low-cost vehicle gives the user the capacity to meet a range of transport needs, and provides a degree of control which is not possible when he has to depend on a hire service. However, the benefits of low-cost vehicles are not restricted to those who own them. The Indian study illustrates the extent to which bullock carts are hired out to village people who do not own a cart, most commonly on a non-cash basis. The trimobiles in the Philippines offer a transport service which in terms of charges is at least competitive with the more conventional vehicles. Furthermore, trimobiles provide a more flexible, widely dispersed service, operating in areas where there are no jeepneys, because they can be used in poor route conditions. Being small and low-cost, they can operate profitably in areas where there is insufficient demand to justify using a jeepney.

Despite the extent of their use, low-cost forms of transport are largely ignored by conventional transport planning with its focus on the national system of engineered roads and conventional motor transport services. Low-cost vehicles lack official 'visibility' and are to a large extent excluded from vehicle statistics. Yet the clear implication from the case studies is that low-cost vehicles and the local transport system to which they belong must be an important element of any transport policy aimed at meeting the needs of rural communities.

2.4 Vehicle ownership

The studies emphasize the low levels of vehicle ownership, and several reported on the income constraints on people's ability both to purchase vehicles and to pay the fares charged by the transport services that were offered. The results from India confirmed earlier findings of the very low level of vehicle ownership. Some 74 per cent of households do not own any form of vehicle, with only some 17 and 9 per cent owning respectively an animal cart or bicycle. At the lowest levels of income, however, the studies show that it is the bicycle which most people would aspire to rather than animal carts. The study in Malaysia reported 13 per cent of households as owning no vehicle at all and a further 32 per cent as owning only a bicycle. In the Nigerian study 32 per cent of the households owned an animal used for transport, and 68 per cent a bicycle: only about 27 per cent of households had some form of motorized transport. Another Indian study indicated that nearly

40 per cent of rural households spend no money on travel or transport.[10]

Even where money is available to purchase motorized vehicles there are other constraints on their acquisition. In the Tanzanian study it was reported that there were more than eight applicants for every motor vehicle on offer. This is a notable example of what is becoming an increasingly common problem for many of the poorer developing countries: foreign exchange limitations on the supply of (imported) motor vehicles. The same constraint applies to the import of spare parts and fuel. The implication is that for these countries the development of efficient non-motorized means of movement that utilize, exclusively or mainly, indigenous resources will necessarily become a major priority.

The inability to obtain credit was, however, the most commonly noted constraint to the acquisition of any type of vehicle, motorized or non-motorized. The study in Kenya attributed the high proportion of second-hand and cash-purchased vehicles as being due to this factor. It is significant that in India well-intentioned government efforts to provide finance specifically for vehicle purchase were being frustrated by defective implementation, principally excessively bureaucratic procedures and indifferent loan administrators. A similar picture emerges from the study in Malaysia, although there had been some impact as far as the development of motor-cycle repair shops. In Nigeria, commercial loans were out of the question for small farmers and the government credit scheme was too limited and too restrictive. The implication here is not that credit schemes don't work. Rather they need to be more flexible to respond to the demand.

3 Towards a more rational approach

In the Introduction we suggested that this book served two main purposes. One was to improve understanding of rural transport needs, the second was to move towards the definition of practical policies to meet these needs. Naturally, these two objectives are inter-related — to develop effective policy one needs a clear definition of the transport demand. The studies go some way to providing this and the conclusions can be summarized as follows:

1. The majority of transport movements in the rural areas are unrelated to agricultural marketing and are made for a whole range of other activities.
2. For most small farmers, the major transport need is for efficient means of transporting small loads over relatively short distances.

3 Short-distance trips within and around the village or community make up the routine transport movements of rural households. Long-distance trips outside the community are much less frequent.
4 Trips for social and welfare activities are a significant proportion of these longer trips made outside the community. The siting of essential services thus influences the nature of rural transport.
5 There is a large range of low-cost means of transport. Many of them are specifically adapted to the locale where they exist. Equally, many of them could be adapted for use in other parts of the world. In nearly all cases, they could be improved. The existence of these means of transport is generally unrelated to the development of a conventional rural road network. It can, however, be argued that in some cases they have developed in response to the lack of conventional roads.

These conclusions seem to suggest that conventional transport planning does not fully address the scope of the problem. The planning and development of rural transport facilities is currently dominated by the provision of engineered roads. Rural transport is planned as if the end of a road into a rural area were the end of the transport system. The road element, however, is only one part of the transport system. Moreover, as the studies show, the majority of rural personal and goods movements do not take place on a road system in the generally accepted sense. Viewed from the perspective of the rural household, the road system is a long way down a transport chain that starts in their field and home. The local level transport system, with which they are familiar, is the other part of the system of which we know too little. Over the past years strenuous efforts have been made to expand the size of the rural road network. Special attention has been paid to reducing construction costs so as to make the money go further. In particular, it has been shown technically and economically feasible to construct roads using labour-based techniques thus reducing the cost and putting money into rural areas. There is no doubt that a more extensive rural road network would be beneficial to development in most developing countries. Nevertheless, the hard fact is that the resources available for the expansion and improvement of rural road networks are limited and in the current difficult economic situation, most governments find the greatest difficulty in maintaining the existing network.

The studies, themselves, particularly those in India and Nigeria, reflect the financial impracticability of providing road access to the mass of the rural population. If it is assumed, as has been the case to date, that this is the only means by which local level transport can be improved, then, of course, the conclusion is a depressing one. If, on the other hand, it is recognized that conventional road transport is only the final link in the whole rural transport system, there is less reason for discouragement although present policies must be reoriented to incorporate the local level system.[11] There must necessarily be a move towards greater emphasis on socio-economic factors in transport appraisal and greater efforts to understand the nature of local level transport needs. Policies related to the local transport system could be defined so as to result in interventions that will bring about improvements in the level of the basic social and economic services of the community and/or region. These interventions should be low-cost and sustainable.

The conclusions imply that, if we are to address seriously the transport needs of the rural population, changes of attitude and of policy will be necessary. Perhaps the most fundamental change required is that footpaths and tracks and simple methods of movement are recognized as legitimate and essential elements of the rural transport system and equally worthy of attention as engineered roads and motor vehicles. The provision of rural transport facilities needs to be viewed in terms of overcoming the constraints and alleviating the problems faced by rural households. This also means that it will be necessary to place an economic value on improvements in the local transport system and that methodologies for doing this must be developed.[12, 13]

The starting point for the planning of rural transport improvements should be the analysis of specific local level movement needs at the rural household or community level. This analysis should not be restricted to the needs of agricultural production but should include the whole range of economic and social activities. Unless subsistence movement requirements are identified and plans made to meet them more efficiently than at present, there is likely to be a serious limitation to the contribution that some family members can make to productive farming and thus to the most likely source of future household wealth. Hitherto there have been few development programmes that have included an element of investment specifically for measures to reduce the drudgery associated with the movement element of subsistence tasks.

Analysis of the range of transport needs should lead to the identification, from a range of possible measures, of the most effective way of utilizing scarce resources to overcome critical transport constraints An important consideration would be the location and supply of social and welfare services which can significantly influence the longer distance transport requirements of communities. The trade-offs between the cost of providing additional social/welfare facilities and that of moving community members to existing service points ought to be an inherent part of any local level development appraisal.

Present policies which emphasize the provision of infrastructure should be broadened to include the possibility of constructing and improving tracks and paths to allow the more efficient operation of low-cost means of transport. Such facilities lend themselves to construction and maintenance by local labour.

A crucial aspect of the more comprehensive approach outlined here is a greater public sector involvement in the vehicle element of rural transport. It may seem incongruous to suggest that the public sector, i.e. government, becomes involved in what is essentially a private sector activity. In terms of national development however such involvement could be quite rational. Previously governments (and aid agencies) have been concerned with investing public funds in road construction to facilitate social and economic development. What is suggested here is that it is in the public interest to facilitate the purchase and use of low-cost vehicles. There is at present no individual capacity in the rural areas to develop these low-cost modes of transport. It will be necessary therefore to promote the transfer of successful low-cost vehicle technologies between countries and, in some cases, even within the same country. Although such transfers do take place through the private sector, they are usually concerned with technologies that are relatively high cost and likely to attract the interest of organizations familiar with international practices and trading. Since many of the potentially most useful technologies are low-cost and offer more limited profit potential, they are most likely to appeal to the small businessman who, paradoxically, cannot be expected to discover and exploit them unaided. This is clearly a situation in which international development agencies and governments should intervene to demonstrate possibilities and thus stimulate local interest and manufacture.

The provision of technical and financial assistance for the local manufacture of efficient low-cost vehicles and of improved traditional devices is an obvious sphere of activity for government and aid agency-sponsored small industry support organizations.

Finally, but of crucial importance in facilitating widespread availability of low-cost vehicles, there is a need to establish innovative credit schemes that provide the modest amounts of finance needed for their purchase, on terms that do not preclude participation by small farmers.

4 Transport and development

The studies illustrate the important role of transport in rural life and in economic and social development. The Kenyan, Tanzanian and Samoan studies provide specific evidence of inadequate transport as a constraint on agricultural production and marketing and indicate how this problem becomes greater with the need to increase farm outputs. However, perhaps the most valuable aspect of the studies is that they show the important role of the local transport system in meeting the people's movement needs and how, for many communities, major transport constraints exist at the local level. The picture which the studies provide of the importance and nature of local level transport needs is very different from that implied by the structure and focus of past rural development investments with their emphasis on long-distance motorized means of movement.

The rationale for conventional rural transport planning is, and has been, economic. It would certainly be irresponsible to propose an alternative approach which was purely social in emphasis and which did not take account of the economic facts of life. It is our contention, however, that the approach outlined above does make economic sense. Improvements to the local transport system would not merely provide access to essential social services. They would also reduce the drudgery of, and the time spent on, basic domestic and farming activities. Consequently, more time and effort could be put into productive, income-generating activities. Moreover, the size of investments required to effect an increase in productivity and output would be relatively small compared with other infrastructure investments. More important, the investments would be more manageable and would be within the control of the people who would benefit from them.

Whilst the economic rationale for low-cost transport investments remains to be proven,[12] the indications from the studies are that a more rational approach to rural transport planning is not only socially desirable but economically viable.

References

Editors' Introduction

1. G. Wilson et al., *The Impact of Highway Investment on Development*, (Washington, D.C., The Brookings Institution, 1966).
2. G.A. Edmonds, 'Towards More Rational Rural Road Transport Planning', in *International Labour Review*, (Geneva, ILO), Jan.-Feb. 1982.
3. I.J. Barwell, G.K. Hathway and J.D.G.F. Howe, *Guide to Low-cost Vehicles for Rural Communities in Developing Countries*, (Vienna, United Nations Industrial Development Organization, October 1982).
4. S. Carapetis, H.L. Beenhakker and J.D.G.F. Howe, The Supply and Quality of Rural Transport Services: A Comparative Review. *World Bank Staff Working Papers, No. 654*, Washington D.C., 1984.
5. G.A. Edmonds and J.J. de Veen, *Road Maintenance: Options for Improvement*, World Employment Programme. (Geneva, ILO, August 1982; mimeographed).
6. World Bank, *The Road Maintenance Problem and International Assistance*, (Washington, D.C., December 1981).
7. Three of the studies, on Malaysia, the Philippines and India, have been published in their original, full length form and are available from the Technology and Employment Branch, ILO, Geneva.

Chapter 2

1. N.S. Ramaswamy: *The Management of Animal Energy Resources and the Modernization of the Bullock-cart system* (Bangalore, Indian Institute of Management 1979).
2. The Government has initiated a Programme (Minimum Needs Plan) to progressively 'connect' villages by all-weather roads as follows:

— villages with 1,500+ population by 1990;
— villages with 1,000-1,500 population, 50 per cent connected by 1990; and
— 50 per cent of the above programme to be completed by 1985.

Such a programme would involve construction of nearly 250,000 km of road costing Rs34,000 million (US$3,500 million in 1978 prices) and in 1990 would still leave over 60 per cent of all villages, mainly those with less than 1,000 population, without an all-weather road connection. The connection of all villages would require construction of nearly 1.3 million km of road and cost Rs180,000 million (1978 prices) or approximately US$20 billion. (Source: Government of India, *Report of the National Transport Policy Committe*, May 1980.)

Chapter 3

1 The numbers of trips made for recreational/social purposes appear to be very low. However this is probably a result of the wording of the survey questionnaire. The relevant question referred specifically to trips to attend festivals or celebrations. No information was sought on other recreational trips.
2 From a literature survey of factors influencing agricultural outputs of Nigerian farmers, and from discussions with Government Agricultural Field Officers and a cross-section of the farmers before the questionnaires were actually prepared.

Chapter 4

1 Government of Kenya: *Development Plan 1979-84*, Parts I and II. (Nairobi, 1979).

Chapter 5

1 K.G. Wright: *Food Marketing within Western Samoa: The Primary Produce Component*, Economic Analysis and Planning Division working paper, (Department of Agriculture, 1976).
2 It is noteworthy that the bicycle is quite rare in the rural areas, and is certainly not the important means of rural transport that it is in many African and Asian countries. Typical travel distances are quite high, and the humid,

high-rainfall climate and undulating terrain in many rural areas are not conducive to cycling.

Chapter 6

1 Backloading devices however do exist in other mountainous areas of the world such as Switzerland and Nepal.
2 The staff is fundamental to one of the *chee-geh's* main features, its self-loading capability. The load that a person is physically capable of carrying on their head or back is much greater than can normally be lifted in position unaided. (On Asian construction sites where headloading in baskets, or metal pans, is the preferred method of moving sand, mortar, etc. it is normal to employ a loader). The staff enables the *chee-geh* to be propped up whilst it is loaded by the carrier who then 'climbs into' the shoulder harness and departs unaided. The staff is carried as a balancing aid and to enable the carrier to stop on route for a rest: the *chee-geh* is simply propped with the staff and the carrier can then 'climb out of' the harness.

Chapter 7

1 It is estimated, however, that per hectare yield has tripled in areas which have been provided with improved access and pump irrigation.
2 Depreciation costs for a trimobile costing P13,000 would be P7-9 per day, leaving P8-10 for maintenance, repair and taxes.
3 *National Transportation Planning Project: Interim Report on Southern Luzon*, (Manila, 1981).

Chapter 8

1 World Bank: *Staff Appraisal Report, Tanzania Pyrethrum Project*, (Washington, March 1980; mimeographed).
2 Twice a week to Lupila; four times a week to Bulongwa.
3 A group of villages south-west of Bulongwa have been saving to purchase a 7-ton truck. The contributions required are:

— Individual T.Sh. 150
— Village council T.Sh. 3,000
— School T.Sh. 500
— Church T.Sh. 250

Between one-third and one-half of the total cost of T.Sh.300,000 has to be saved before a loan can be raised through the Ministry of Rural Development. Another scheme has been initiated under the Ward Secretary in which Kijombo village is located. Individual contributions are just T.Shs.20, but only T.Shs.2,800 has been saved and morale is admitted to be low.
4 G. Glaister: 'The Self-help Approach, Afghanistan', in G.A. Edmonds and J.D.G.F. Howe (Eds.): *Roads and Resources: Appropriate Technology in Road Construction and Maintenance in Developing Countries*, (ILO, Geneva, 1980)

Chapter 9

1 Government of Bangladesh: Country Paper prepared for the ESCAP meeting on the improvement of non-motorized transport, (Bangkok, 8-14 March 1983.)
2 The biases this gives rise to have only recently been acknowledged and are eloquently described by R. Chambers 'Rural Poverty Unperceived: Problems and Remedies' in *World Development* 1980.
3 A 'union' is an administrative division of a *thana*.
4 These non-mechanized boats are the most important form of rural transport in riverine areas of the country.

Chapter 10

1 For example, 2-3 tonnes of water are required during the year to spray 0.5 ha of cotton — a formidable amount if headloading is used for transport.
2 Ministry of Transport and Communications: *Trends in Road Use in Kenya*, (Nairobi, July 1971)
3 This is supported by the evidence from Kaira's study in Chapter 4.
4 ILO: *Employment, Incomes and Equality in Kenya*, (Geneva, 1972).
5 This figure is dated, and does not give a complete picture because since that survey money earned by family members working in towns has become a significant element of rural household incomes. A more recent survey revealed an average total family income in the smallholder sector of K.Sh.5,000-7,000 (US$590-830).

Chapter 11

1 Report of the National Transport Planning Committee, Government of India, May 1980.
2 El-Hawary, M.A. and El-Reedy, T.Y. *Rural Roads and Poverty Alleviation in Egypt*, (Geneva, ILO, 1982).
3 Carapetis, S., Beenhakker, H.L. and Howe, J.D.G.F.: The Supply and Quality of Rural Transport Services: A Comparative Review. *World Bank Staff Working Papers No. 654,* Washington D.C., 1984.
4 *Philippine Islands Roads Feasibility Study: Final Report (general text)*, Ministry of Public Highways: (Manila, 1980)
5 Hall, D.D.: 'Biomass for Energy: Fuels Now and in the Future', in *Journal of the Royal Society of Arts*, July 1982. No. 5312, CXXX, page 457-471.
6 Cook, C.: *Rural Mobility and Communications in Mexico: Interim Report*, (Washington D.C., World Bank, March 1981 (mimeographed).
7 Van der Wees, G.: *Mobility, Transportation and Economic Development in Rural Areas of Developing Nations: Perspectives from Tanzania*, (Seattle, University of Washington, November 1978).
8 Bureau of Highways of Ministry of Communications. *China Non-Motorized Vehicles*, People's Republic of China, 1983.
9 Thorburn, C., Darrow, K. and Stannky, B.: *Teknologi Kampungan: A Collection of Indigenous Indonesian Technologies*, Appropriate Technology Project of Volunteers in Asia, June 1983.
10 Madhavan, S.: *Rural Transport in Karnataka with Special Reference to Kanakapura, Bangalore District, India*. Research Working Paper No. 7, School of Social Sciences and Business Studies, Polytechnic of Central London, July 1980.
11 Edmonds, G.A.: 'Towards More Rational Rural Road Transport Planning', in *International Labour Review*, (Geneva, ILO) Vol. 121, No. 1, Jan.-Feb. 1982.
12 Howe, J.D.: *A Conceptual Framework for Defining and Evaluating Improvement to Local Level Rural Transport in Developing Communities*, September 1983, (Geneva, mimeographed).
13 Kaira, C.: *Transportation Needs of the Rural Population in Developing Countries*, (Institut für Regionalwissenschaft de Universität Karlsruhe, April 1983).

Selected Bibliography

W. Owen, *Strategy for Mobility*. (Washington, DC, The Brookings Institution, 1964).

G. Wilson et al., *The Impact of Highway Investment on Development*. (Washington, DC, The Brookings Institution, 1966).

W. Owen, *Distance and Development*. (Washington, DC, The Brookings Institution, 1968).

B.S. Hoyle (ed.), *Transport and Development*. (London, Macmillan, 1973).

R. Hofmeier, *Transport and Economic Development in Tanzania*. (Munchen, Weltforum Verlag, 1973).

World Bank, *Comparative Evaluation of Selected Highway Projects*, Operations Evaluation Department Report No. 349. (Washington, DC, 1974).

P. Blaikie, J. Cameron and D. Seddon, *The Effects of Roads in West Central Nepal*. (Overseas Development Group, University of East Anglia, 1977).

G. van der Wees, *Mobility, Transportation and Economic Development in Rural Areas of Developing Countries: Perspectives from Tanzania*. (Seattle, University of Washington, November 1978).

I.J. Barwell and J.D. Howe, *Appropriate Transport Facilities for the Rural Sector in Developing Countries*. (Vienna, UNIDO, and Geneva, ILO, 1979).

S. Madhavan, *Rural Transport in Karnataka with Special Reference to Kanakapura, Bangalore District, India*, Research Working Paper. (School of Social Sciences and Business Studies, Polytechnic of Central London, July 1980).

J. Bugnicourt et al., *Transports en Sursis?* (Enda Dakar, Senegal, March 1981).

C. Cook, *Rural Mobility and Communications in Mexico: Interim Report*, Transportation and Water Department. (Washington, DC, World Bank, March 1981).

World Bank, *The Road Maintenance Problem and International Assistance*. (Washington, DC, December 1981).

G.A. Edmonds and J.J. de Veen, *Road Maintenance: Options for*

Improvement. (Geneva, World Employment Programme, ILO, August 1982, mimeographed).

R.B. Ocampo, *Low-cost Transport in Asia: A Comparative Report on Five Cities*. (Ottawa, Canada, International Development Research Centre, 1982).

S. Carapetis, H.L. Beenhakker and J.D.G.F. Howe, The Supply and Quality of Rural Transport Services: A Comparative Review. *World Bank Staff Working Papers No. 654*, Washington, D.C., 1984.

I.J. Barwell, G.K. Hathway and J.D.G.F. Howe, *Guide to Low-cost Vehicles for Rural Communities in Developing Countries*. (Vienna, UNIDO, October 1982).

J.D.G.F. Howe, *A Conceptual Framework for Defining and Evaluating Improvement to Local Level Rural Transport in Developing Communities*. (Geneva, ILO, September 1983; mimeographed).

World Bank, *Transportation Sector Strategy Support Paper*. (Washington, DC, 1983).

J.D.G.F. Howe and P. Richards (eds.), *Rural Roads and Poverty Alleviation*. (London, I.T. Publications, 1984).